HOMEMADE
MADE EASY
COOKBOOK

by **TINA VERRELLI**

Author, Tina Verrelli; Editors, Jodi Flayman, Merly Mesa, Carol Ginsburg; Recipe Development and Food Styling, Patty Rosenthal and Tina Verrelli; Photographers, Kelly Rusin and Freedom Martinez; Post Production, Hal Silverman of Hal Silverman Studio; Cover and Page Design, Lorraine Dan of Grand Design.

The paper in this printing meets the requirements of the ANSI Standard Z39.48-1992.

While every care has been taken in compiling the recipes for this book, the publisher, Cogin, Inc., or any other person who has been involved in working on this publication assumes no responsibility or liability for any errors or omissions, inadvertent or not, that may be found in the recipes or text, nor for any problems or damages that may arise as a result of preparing these recipes.

If food allergies or dietary restrictions are a concern, it is recommended that you carefully read ingredient product labels as well as consult a nutritionist or your physician to determine if a recipe meets your dietary needs.

We encourage you to use caution when working with all kitchen equipment and to always follow food safety guidelines.

To purchase this book for business or promotional use or to purchase more than 50 copies at a discount, or for custom editions, please contact Cogin, Inc. at the address below.

Inquiries should be addressed to:

Cogin, Inc.

1770 NW 64 Street, Suite 500

Fort Lauderdale, FL 33309

ISBN: 978-0-9981635-9-8

Printed in the United States of America

First Edition

Foreword

My friends would always joke that they only came to my house for the food. The minute they stepped through the door, it only took one whiff and they knew what my mom was cooking. Whether it was Bundt cake or pulled pork, the overwhelming smell of amazing food traveled throughout the house, as though it was fanned straight from the plate to our noses.

Dinner was never anything boring in the Verrelli household. Going to my friends' houses for dinner was always a big wake up call. Even going to restaurants, I'd question, where's the flavor? Where are the spices, the creativity, the personality in the food? Every time I came home, I was happy to be welcomed by my mom's cooking.

My mom has always experimented in the kitchen. Early on, she was always entering a new recipe contest, often winning, and yes, sometimes losing. (In which case, of course, I disagreed with the judges' decisions.) Later on, she started creating recipes for her blog, *epicuricloud*. Now, she continues to create recipes to demonstrate on QVC. Through this process, there have been amazing, uniquely-crafted recipes that she continues to make today, and that I will use when I have my own family to cook for. There have also been a lot of recipes that my sister, dad and I had to critique at the dinner table, sometimes with scorecards! (I have a particularly scarring memory of a sandwich featuring cantaloupe).

When recipes didn't work out right away, my mom tweaked them as many times as needed until they were just right. A few months ago, my mom was testing a cinnamon pie recipe, and it took her five tries before she deemed it perfect. I was satisfied with the pie after the first try. Let's just say, we ate a lot of pie that month.

On the days we aren't running in different directions, keeping up with our busy schedules, we eat together as a family. Hearing my mom call "Dinnerrr!" up the stairs is one of the greatest sounds ever. I know that I can expect something delicious, new and exciting.

I hope you find this book, which is filled with many of these recipes, not only something to be read and referenced, but something that you'll want to pass down and share. My mom's years of hard work and creativity are embedded in these pages, and you can trust that her recipes will turn out great every time. You have my word; they're tried and true.

Sam Verrelli,
Tina's Daughter

Welcome

For those of you who don't know me, my name is Tina Verrelli and I'm a busy mom, wife, food blogger, KitchenAid® presenter on QVC, former elementary school teacher, and now...a cookbook author! (It's not always easy wearing all of these hats,

but it sure is fun!) While this is my very first cookbook, I've been creating and sharing my own recipes for close to a decade now. I couldn't be more excited for you to have all of my favorites close at hand.

My recipes offer a little something for everyone. You'll find from-scratch recipes for those days when you have a little extra time, as well as semi-homemade recipes for when you really just want to get dinner on the table...fast. Some recipes are on the healthy side, while others are meant to be once-in-a-while treats. I'm all about offering you options, so that you enjoy your time in the kitchen as much as I do. (This was my inspiration for the title, Homemade Made Easy!)

If you're an "all-day breakfast" kind of eater, you're going to love the chapter on morning favorites, including my Rise & Shine Sweet Potato Bake or Strawberry Shortcake Waffles. For those of you who love that "stick-to-your-ribs" feeling, then wait till you taste my Cornbread Taco Casserole or my Slow Cooker Sausage & Bean One-Pot. They're both packed with flavor and sure to leave you feeling happily full!

Along with lots of family-friendly, weeknight dinner ideas, I've included a bunch of recipes that are perfect for feeding a crowd. Not only did I grow up in a large family (I'm the youngest of six!), but I'm a big fan of hosting holiday events and special dinners for all of my friends and neighbors. (Ask my husband, there are often 30 people or more at any one of these occasions!) That's why you'll find some of my favorite dips, sliders, wings, and poppers—they are perfect for sharing!

Don't worry, there are plenty of treats to satisfy your sweet tooth too. How about a tried-and-true favorite like My Mom's Homemade Brownies or an ultra-decadent slice of Mattison Avenue Toffee Cheesecake? (It's okay if you go ahead and skip to the dessert chapter first!)

I understand what it means to be a busy home cook, which is why I've made things as easy as possible for you. Not only are my recipe instructions simple to follow, but you'll be able to find all of the ingredients you need at most grocery stores. (You may even have a lot of them at home already!) Plus, there are tips on almost every recipe to inspire you with ideas for presentation, substitutions for taste, or tricks for making things even easier.

And because I find photos of food to be almost as inspiring as the stories behind the dishes, I made sure that there is plenty of delicious photography throughout this cookbook. I hope it serves to tempt you, inspire you, and guide you, whenever necessary. (Confession: sometimes I like to flip through cookbooks just for the photos!)

While adding "cookbook author" to my list of life's accomplishments is a dream come true, it wouldn't have been possible without the support of all of my family, friends, and lovely viewers on the "Q". Thank you for being a part of my journey and for allowing me to share my very favorite recipes with you. This is only the beginning, and I look forward to creating new recipes and sharing them with you for a long time. I hope you enjoy the recipes and the memories they become a part of. And if you will, please let me know which of these are your favorites and if they brought your family and friends as much joy as they did mine. To me, there's nothing more wonderful than hearing about how people have enjoyed my food.

This collage is a small snapshot of so many wonderful cooking experiences that I am happy to share with you. When I look back at these photos, they bring back so many great memories, and fill my heart with joy.

Some Thoughts & Helpful Tips

Before we get started, I want to share a few of my thoughts that I take into consideration whenever I'm creating a recipe. These simple things are what I believe turn good recipes into memorable ones.

- **Low-Sodium Broth:** When using store-bought beef or chicken broth in a recipe, I often suggest using the low-sodium versions. I've learned that you can always add more salt to a dish before serving it, but you can't take it out. Plus, it allows you to taste all the other flavors and helps develop your palate.

- **Fresh vs. Powdered Garlic and Onion:** When it comes to adding garlic and onions to a recipe, I always prefer to add fresh, rather than garlic or onion powder. On occasion you'll see that I do add these in the powdered form, which can be a real time saver.

- **Oven Thermometer:** Always check your oven temperature with a separate oven thermometer. They are inexpensive and can be purchased wherever kitchen supplies are sold. I keep one in my oven all the time to make sure I always preheat to the correct temperature. (I love mine, as it saved me when one of my ovens had been off by at least 25 degrees.)

- **Cheesecake Crust:** To help prevent your cheesecake crust from getting soggy, you can prebake it at 350 degrees for 10 minutes. Let cool before adding your filling. This is especially helpful when making your cheesecake a day or two in advance.

- **Dark Baking Sheets:** When baking using glass or dark colored baking pans and baking sheets, you may want to reduce your oven temperature by 25 degrees. The darker pans can cause your baked goods to bake and brown more quickly. (My exception to this rule is when baking pies and pizzas – I want all that nice browning to happen!)

- **Foil Sling:** You may have noticed I like to use a foil or parchment paper sling in my baking pans when baking brownies and bars. (See pages 204-206.) I love to be able to lift the whole bar out of the pan when cool; it's much easier to cut and serve neater bars.

- **Electric Knife for Desserts:** Speaking of cutting neater bars ... When I use a sling and my bars are on a cutting board, I love to use my electric knife to cut very neat squares — especially when there are nuts and chips to cut through. Plus, it's fun to use power tools in the kitchen!

- **Measuring Flour:** The most precise way to measure flour is to weigh it, but since not everyone has a kitchen scale, I suggest spooning flour into your measuring cup and leveling it off with a straight-edged knife. (Don't pack it or shake it to level.) Incorrectly measuring flour can add as much as 16% extra flour to a recipe.

- **Softened Butter:** When a recipe calls for softened butter, the butter should still be cool to the touch (about 65 degrees F) and when you press on it, it should make a slight indentation, but not squish into the butter. Leaving refrigerated butter out for 30 minutes usually does the trick. You can cut it up into pieces if you want the butter to soften a little more quickly. It is better to start with butter that's too cold than to use partially melted butter. While you are softening your butter, leave your eggs out too! Eggs combine better when at room temperature.

- **Creaming:** Creaming butter and sugar (and sometimes cream cheese) is very important to the texture of a recipe. When you cream ingredients together, you add air to the mixture which will give structure to cakes and cookies. The butter should be softened, but not too soft. (See tip above.) The butter needs to be able to accept and hold air. The process of creaming presses the sugar granules into the butter creating air pockets. When butter and sugar are properly creamed it will look fluffy and lighter in color. It usually takes more time than you would think — so don't skimp on the creaming.

- **Salted Butter vs. Unsalted Butter:** What's the difference? About ¼ teaspoon of salt per stick. So if you need to substitute one, either way, you can just take out or add in a little salt to the recipe.

- **Brown Sugar Hard as a Rock?** When your brown sugar is beyond repair, make your own! In your chopper or food processor, mix together 1 cup of granulated sugar and 2 tablespoons of molasses. Voila!

- **Hand Mixer vs. Stand Mixer:** People often ask me how to know whether to use a stand mixer or a hand mixer. Sometimes they are interchangeable, however a stand mixer allows you to have both your hands free without holding a mixer in one of them. Plus, a stand mixer is ideal if you're mixing, whipping or kneading something for a longer period of time. There are also many attachments you can use with your stand mixer to get the most out of your investment. (ie: Ice Cream Bowl, Spiralizer, Pasta Roller...) If you're wondering which one to purchase, think about your needs and habits before you make the purchase. Most people first buy a hand mixer, then purchase a stand mixer when they want to start cooking and baking more often or when it fits their budget.

  » **Hand Mixers:** A hand mixer is a kitchen must have. Even people who don't cook or bake very often are quick to discover how handy this kitchen essential is. Not only will it save you time, it will do a better job of mixing cake batter or cookie dough, it will mash potatoes, whip butter or cream, and beat eggs in minutes. Hand mixers are lightweight and portable. They can be taken to the job; I find it handy to mash potatoes right in the pot or shred chicken right in my slow cooker. All hand mixers come with a pair of removable, all-purpose metal beaters. Most models also include a whisk or dough hook attachment, and all of them have several speeds which makes them very versatile.

  » **Stand Mixers:** Like hand mixers, most stand mixers come with several useful beater accessories, including a dough hook, wire whip, flat beater and sometimes even a flex-edge beater. If you love to make things like layer cakes, buttercream or homemade bread, then a stand mixer will certainly make your life easier. You'll be able to focus on other tasks as your stand mixer whips buttercream or kneads bread dough. It's a real time saver. Even the best home bakers don't always mix ingredients long enough when using a hand mixer, so a stand mixer may even improve the quality of your baked goods or inspire you to try something new!

- **Dry vs. Liquid Measurements:** Here's a common cooking question—how many ounces in a cup? Unfortunately, the answer isn't as simple as it seems. Fluid ounces and measured weight are very different, so let me help you out.

  Liquid measuring cups indicate that 1 cup = 8 ounces. But what they really mean is 1 cup of liquid = 8 fluid ounces. For dry measurements, the rules change. Because dry ingredients vary greatly in weight, you can't rely on the same conversion. For example, 1 cup of all-purpose flour weighs 4.5 ounces, not 8 ounces. On the other hand, 1 cup of chocolate chips weighs a little over 6 ounces.

  To keep things easy, throughout this book, if a recipe calls for a cup measure, grab your measuring cup and fill it as it as the recipe suggests. On the other hand, if the recipe calls for, let's say 8 ounces of frozen corn, you would use an 8 ounce bag of corn or half a 16 ounce bag.

  There are two main types of measuring cups—dry measuring cups and liquid measuring cups—and it matters which one you use. Dry measuring cups are designed to measure dry ingredients like flour, nuts, and berries, while liquid measuring cups are designed to measure liquids like water, cooking oil, and yogurt.

  Liquid measuring cups are usually glass or plastic with a pour spout and a handle. They allow you to pour a liquid into the cup and bring it even with a measurement line without spilling. Dry measuring cups, on the other hand, hold the exact amount of an ingredient and should be leveled off with a flat edge.

  Using the right type of measuring cup can determine the outcome of the recipe you're making.

  Here's a good rule of thumb to follow—when measuring dry ingredients, use dry measuring cups or weigh the ingredients with a scale. For liquids, stick to a liquid measuring cup.

Some Helpful Equivalent Measures

A pinch --- just less than ⅛ teaspoon

3 teaspoons --------------------------------------- 1 tablespoon

2 tablespoons liquid --------------------------- 1 fluid ounce

4 tablespoons ----------------------------------- ¼ cup or 2 fluid ounces

1 cup liquid --------------------------------------- 8 fluid ounces

2 cups liquid ------------------------------------- 1 pint ---------------------------------½ quart

4 quarts -- 1 gallon

1 tablespoon butter ----------------------------- ⅛ stick -----------------------------------½ ounce

2 tablespoons butter --------------------------- ¼ stick ------------------------------------1 ounce

4 tablespoons butter --------------------------- ½ stick ------------------------------------2 ounces

8 tablespoons butter --------------------------- 1 stick -------------------------------------4 ounces

1 cup uncooked rice + 2 cups liquid------------ 3 cups cooked rice

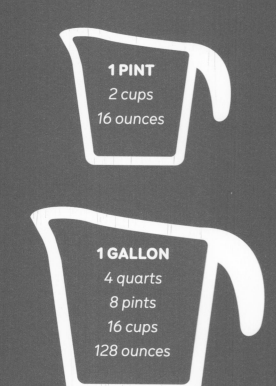

1 PINT

2 cups

16 ounces

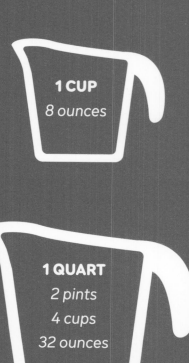

1 CUP

8 ounces

1 GALLON

4 quarts

8 pints

16 cups

128 ounces

1 QUART

2 pints

4 cups

32 ounces

Table
of Contents

Foreword iii

Welcome iv

Some Thoughts and Helpful Tips viii

Equivalent Measures xii

Breakfast & Brunch 1

Appetizers & Starters 25

Soups, Salads, & Sandwiches 55

Chicken & Turkey 81

Beef & Pork 105

Seafood, Pasta, & More 131

Sides 161

Dessert 191

Index 230

Breakfast & Brunch

Pecan Streusel French Toast Cups.. 2

Spiralized Sweet Potato Bake.. 4

Greek Isles Breakfast Wraps... 6

Hearty Ham & Potato Hash.. 7

Avocado Toast Eggs Benedict... 8

Asparagus & Bacon Cheesy Quiche... 10

Fluffy Overnight Cinnamon Rolls 11

Our Favorite Pancakes.. 12

Sweet & Spicy Candied Bacon... 14

Just Peachy Bourbon Spread.. 15

Strawberry Shortcake Waffles.. 16

PB & B Overnight Oats.. 18

Chocolate-Almond Crescent Rollups 19

Lemon-Kissed Raspberry Muffins 20

Tropical Summer Smoothie.. 22

Strawberry Sunrise Smoothie... 22

Pecan Streusel French Toast Cups

Makes 12

6 eggs

1-¾ cups milk

¼ teaspoon salt

2 teaspoons vanilla

1 teaspoon cinnamon

2 tablespoons brown sugar

12 to 15 slices white bread

Pecan Streusel

⅓ cup brown sugar

½ teaspoon cinnamon

2 tablespoons all-purpose flour

3 tablespoons cold butter

½ cup finely chopped pecans

Tina's Tip: *If you have a few left over, simply reheat them on a baking sheet in a 300 degree oven for about 10 minutes or until hot.*

1 Coat a 12-cup muffin tin with cooking spray.

2 In a large bowl, whisk together eggs, milk, salt, vanilla, 1 teaspoon cinnamon, and 2 tablespoons brown sugar. Pour about 2 tablespoons egg mixture into each muffin cup.

3 Cut each slice of bread into 4 quarters. Stack 4 to 5 bread pieces and place the stack cut-side up (so the top looks like a fan) into each muffin cup. (You want the bread to fit snugly in each cup.) Allow them to absorb the egg mixture, then flip each stack, so the "eggy" part is now up. Slowly pour the rest of the egg mixture evenly into all the cups. Cover with plastic wrap and refrigerate 1 hour or overnight.

4 When ready to bake, preheat oven to 350 degrees F. To make the Pecan Streusel, in a small bowl, combine ⅓ cup brown sugar, ½ teaspoon cinnamon, and the flour; mix well. Cut the butter into the sugar mixture using a chopper or pastry blender; stir in the pecans. Evenly divide streusel mixture over the top of each muffin cup.

5 Bake 25 to 30 minutes or until puffed, golden brown, and set in the center. Allow to cool for about 3 minutes, loosen around the edges with a knife, and serve.

My family loves French toast, but with our busy schedules it's not always the most convenient thing to make. That's where this recipe comes to the rescue. You can make these individually-portioned French toast cups the night before and bake them in the morning. They even reheat well, which is great for those mornings when I need to get to QVC and my daughters have their 6 a.m. swim team practices.

Spiralized Sweet Potato Bake

Serves 6 to 8

3 sweet potatoes

2 tablespoons olive oil, divided

1 pound breakfast or sweet Italian turkey sausage

⅓ cup finely chopped onion

½ teaspoon salt, divided

5 ounces baby spinach (about 3-½ cups), roughly chopped

12 eggs

1 cup half-and-half

¼ teaspoon black pepper

1 teaspoon Italian seasoning

½ cup grated Parmesan cheese, divided

¾ cup crumbled feta cheese

Tina's Tip: *This is another great make-ahead breakfast dish. I put everything except the egg mixture in the baking dish the night before. Then in the morning, all I do is pour in the egg mixture, top with the remaining Parmesan cheese, and bake it off. How easy it that?*

1 Preheat oven to 350 degrees F. Coat a 2-½ quart baking dish with cooking spray.

2 Trim ends off sweet potatoes and cut them to fit a spiralizer (if necessary). If you're using a KitchenAid® Spiralizer, use the peeling blade and fine spiralizing blade to peel and spiralize the sweet potatoes. If you're using a manual spiralizer, peel the potatoes before spiralizing. Either way, you should have about 5 cups of sweet potato spirals.

3 In a large skillet over medium heat, heat 1 tablespoon oil until hot. Crumble and cook sausage (make sure you remove any casings) for 5 minutes or until no pink remains. Remove to a paper towel-lined plate. In the same skillet over medium heat, add remaining 1 tablespoon oil and the onion, and cook 1 to 2 minutes or until tender. Sprinkle with ¼ teaspoon salt. Add the spinach and continue to cook, stirring, until spinach wilts.

4 In a medium bowl, whisk together eggs, half-and-half, remaining ¼ teaspoon salt, the black pepper, Italian seasoning, and ¼ cup Parmesan cheese.

5 Arrange sweet potato spirals in baking dish. Top with sausage, spinach mixture, and feta cheese. Pour egg mixture evenly over top and sprinkle with remaining ¼ cup Parmesan cheese. Bake 45 minutes, cover with foil, and cook 15 more minutes or until set in the center.

The Spiralizer is one of my favorite KitchenAid® attachments. If you don't have one you can still enjoy this rise-and-shine sweet potato bake—just use any spiralizer or buy pre-spiralized sweet potatoes at your grocery store. What I love about this dish, besides the delicious flavors, is that it's full of veggies and protein — a great way to start your day!

Greek Isles Breakfast Wraps

Makes 4

8 eggs

2 tablespoons water

¼ teaspoon salt

¼ teaspoon black pepper

1 tablespoon butter

½ cup chopped roasted red peppers, drained well

¼ cup pitted Kalamata olives, sliced

½ cup crumbled feta cheese

½ teaspoon dried oregano

2 cups fresh spinach

4 (8-inch) spinach or plain tortillas

1 In a medium bowl, whisk eggs, water, salt, and pepper.

2 In a large skillet over medium heat, melt butter; add egg mixture and scramble until almost set. Add roasted red peppers, olives, feta cheese, oregano, and spinach; stir gently until combined.

3 Remove from heat and evenly divide egg mixture onto the middle of each tortilla. Fold the edge of the tortilla that's closest to you over the filling, then fold in each side and roll tightly, ending with the seam-side down.

4 Heat panini press according to directions. (See Tip). Place filled tortilla on panini press, cover, and heat 1 to 2 minutes or until heated through. Repeat with remaining tortillas. Cut in half and serve immediately.

Tina's Tip: *I love my panini press, but if you don't have one, no problem. Just grill these in a nonstick skillet or grill pan that's been sprayed with cooking spray. You can replicate the method of a panini press by placing a heavy pan on top of your wrap while it's cooking in the skillet. Flip them when they're golden and repeat.*

Breakfast wraps are a nice break from the typical breakfast sandwich or scrambled eggs and toast, and these are a little bit more special because they're inspired by some of my favorite Greek flavors. I love the combination of olives, spinach, and feta cheese, so coming up with this recipe was a no-brainer. I hope you feel as "whisked away" as I do when I start my day with one of these.

Hearty Ham & Potato Hash

Serves 6 to 8

4 tablespoons butter

¼ cup canola oil

1 large onion, diced

1 (2-pound) bag frozen hash brown potato cubes, thawed

½ teaspoon garlic powder

½ teaspoon black pepper

½ pound (1-½ cups) diced cooked ham (see Tip)

1 In a large skillet over medium heat, melt butter with oil. Add onion and sauté 3 to 4 minutes or until soft.

2 Add hash brown potatoes, garlic powder, and black pepper and cook 15 minutes or until potatoes begin to brown and crisp up.

3 Stir in ham and cook 4 to 6 more minutes or until heated through.

Tina's Tip: *This is a great way to use leftover ham on the holidays. Imagine whipping up a hearty breakfast like this the day after Christmas or Easter. On those days when I'm craving this and there's no leftover ham in the fridge, I head to the deli and pick up a half-pound of thick-cut deli ham.*

We live in an area with a lot of diners, and when we have time, we love to go out for breakfast. When we go on vacation, we always try to check out the local diners where we know we'll find a good breakfast. This recipe was inspired by all those diners and breakfast joints that dot our country and often have a line out the door. It's hearty, it's wholesome, and yes, it's far from guilt-free. My favorite part of this dish is the crispy-crunchy parts of the potatoes!

Avocado Toast Eggs Benedict

Makes 4

3 ripe avocados, halved, pitted, and skin removed

1 tablespoon lemon juice

¼ teaspoon salt

Hollandaise Sauce

3 egg yolks

1 teaspoon Dijon mustard

1 tablespoon lemon juice

3 dashes hot pepper sauce

⅛ teaspoon salt

1 stick butter

Black pepper for sprinkling

4 slices whole-grain bread

4 eggs

1 In a small bowl, mash avocados with a fork until desired consistency. Stir in 1 tablespoon lemon juice and ¼ teaspoon salt; set aside.

2 To make the Hollandaise Sauce, in a blender, combine egg yolks, mustard, 1 tablespoon lemon juice, the hot pepper sauce, and ⅛ teaspoon salt. Cover and blend 5 seconds; set aside. In a microwave-safe bowl, melt butter in microwave 30 to 45 seconds or until melted and hot. With blender running, slowly pour hot butter into yolk mixture and blend until thickened.

3 Toast bread and place each slice on a serving plate. Spread avocado mixture evenly over toast. Pan-fry eggs to desired doneness and place each egg on top of avocado toast. Spoon Hollandaise sauce over eggs, sprinkle with pepper, and enjoy.

My daughter, Sam, loves avocado toast. Normally, she just throws a fried or scrambled egg on top and calls it a day. But since she's a pretty adventurous eater, I once surprised her by adding a homemade Hollandaise sauce. It's definitely an easy way to dress up her favorite.

Asparagus & Bacon Cheesy Quiche

Serves 6 to 8

1 homemade pie crust (see Note) or 1 refrigerated pie crust (from a 14.1-ounce package)

1-½ cups shredded Swiss cheese

1-½ cups shredded cheddar cheese

8 slices bacon

½ cup finely chopped onion

1 cup chopped asparagus

4 eggs

1 cup heavy cream

1 cup milk

¼ teaspoon salt

1 Preheat oven to 375 degrees F. Arrange oven rack to lowest position. (This helps the crust brown on the bottom.)

2 Place pie crust in a 9-inch deep-dish pie plate and flute edges.

3 Sprinkle cheeses evenly into bottom of pie crust; set aside.

4 In a large skillet over medium heat, cook bacon until crisp, remove to a paper towel-lined plate to cool slightly, then crumble. Discard all but 1 tablespoon of bacon drippings. In the same skillet over medium heat, add onion and asparagus, and cook 3 to 4 minutes or until softened. Sprinkle bacon and vegetable mixture over cheese.

5 In a medium bowl, beat eggs, heavy cream, milk, and salt until well blended. Slowly pour over filling in pie crust. Bake 40 to 45 minutes or until center of quiche is just a bit jiggly. Let stand at least 10 minutes to set up, then slice into wedges and serve.

Note: Making your own pie crust is easier than you think. See my recipe on page 215.

10

What I love most about quiche is how easy it is to customize. When it comes to the cheese, feel free to use your favorites by mixing and matching them, as long as you use 3 cups total. You can also swap out the asparagus for some broccoli florets, and even add some sun-dried tomatoes if you'd like. It's all up to you!

Fluffy Overnight Cinnamon Rolls

Makes 12

Cinnamon Filling

6 tablespoons butter, softened

⅓ cup brown sugar

⅓ cup granulated sugar

1 tablespoon cinnamon

¼ teaspoon kosher salt

1 batch sweet dough
(see page 220)

Cream Cheese Icing

4 ounces cream cheese, softened

2 tablespoons butter, softened

½ teaspoon vanilla

1-½ cups powdered sugar

2 to 3 tablespoons milk

Tina's Tip: *If you don't have a warm place for your dough to rise, create one by heating some water, then placing the dough in a cold oven on an upper rack. Place an empty, heat-safe dish on a lower oven rack. Pour a few cups of hot water into the empty dish and close oven door. This creates a warm and steamy dough-rising environment.*

1 In a bowl, mix together Cinnamon Filling ingredients until soft and spreadable. Coat a 9- x 13-inch baking dish with cooking spray.

2 Sprinkle a little flour on a flat surface for rolling. Roll dough into a 12- x 18-inch rectangle. (This dough is very soft; you can actually pat it out with your hands rather than rolling, if you like.) Spread filling mixture evenly over dough, leaving a 1-inch border. Starting with the long side, roll dough with both hands. Place seam-side down and use your hands to even out the roll. With a serrated knife, cut into 12 equal pieces.

3 Place rolls, cut-side down, evenly spaced, in baking dish and cover with plastic wrap that has been coated with cooking spray (coated-side down, so dough doesn't stick to plastic wrap). Refrigerate overnight.

4 In the morning, place baking dish on counter, covered, until rolls come to room temperature, rise, and start getting puffy in the center. (See Tip.) Preheat oven to 350 degrees F. Bake 25 to 30 minutes or until golden brown.

5 Meanwhile, to make the Cream Cheese Icing, with an electric mixer, beat together cream cheese and butter until smooth. Slowly add vanilla and mix in powdered sugar. Add milk, 1 tablespoon at a time, until it reaches a spreadable consistency. Spread icing over warm rolls.

Our Favorite Pancakes

Makes 8 (4-inch) pancakes

¾ cup whole wheat flour

⅓ cup all-purpose flour

2 tablespoons sugar

2 teaspoons baking powder

¼ teaspoon salt

1 cup milk

1 egg

1 teaspoon vanilla

2 tablespoons melted butter, plus extra for buttering griddle

Fresh blueberries, chocolate chips or your favorite pancake mix-ins

1 In a medium bowl, whisk together whole wheat flour, all-purpose flour, sugar, baking powder, and salt. In a small bowl, whisk together milk, egg, and vanilla. Stir milk mixture into dry ingredients. Add melted butter. Mix just until combined. (A few lumps should remain.) Let batter rest 5 minutes.

2 Meanwhile, preheat griddle over medium-low heat. Coat with melted butter. Pour about ¼ cup batter for each pancake onto griddle. Sprinkle each pancake with blueberries, chocolate chips, or your favorite pancake mix-in. Cook pancakes until tops begin to bubble; flip and cook until both sides are golden. Repeat with remaining batter.

Tina's Tip: *Everyone in my family loves these. As a matter of fact my daughter, Lauren, loves when I make these as mini pancakes (or silver dollar-sized). That way, she can dip each pancake into some syrup. If you have kids or teenagers who are big dippers, then you might want to make these mini versions too!*

We're not a pancake versus waffle kind of family; we like them both. However, everyone has their own favorite way of eating them. My daughter, Lauren, loves pancakes plain or with chocolate chips, while my husband and I go for the fresh blueberries. So when you're making these, make sure you find out what everyone likes best. And don't forget to set out the butter and real maple syrup—those are a must!

Sweet & Spicy Candied Bacon

Makes 10 to 12 strips

1 pound thick-cut bacon
(10 to 12 strips)

½ cup brown sugar

1 teaspoon finely ground black pepper

⅛ teaspoon cayenne pepper

½ teaspoon ground ginger

1 Preheat oven to 375 degrees F. Line a rimmed baking sheet with parchment paper or foil. Arrange bacon on baking sheet.

2 In a small bowl, stir together brown sugar, black pepper, cayenne pepper, and ginger. Sprinkle bacon slices with half the sugar mixture.

3 Bake 20 minutes. Remove pan from oven, flip bacon slices, and sprinkle with remaining sugar mixture. Return to oven and bake 10 to 15 more minutes or until bacon is crispy and sugar is caramelized.

4 Remove bacon to a platter lined with parchment or wax paper to cool. Serve at room temperature.

Tina's Tip: *I love baking my bacon. You don't have to worry about bacon grease splatters and it's perfect for making big batches for a crowd. If you like your bacon really crispy, cook your bacon on a wire rack that fits inside a rimmed baking sheet. The rack allows the bacon grease to drip off the slices, ensuring lots of crispy goodness.*

The first time I had candied bacon was on a trip to Key West many, many years ago. We were at a restaurant for brunch and I had never had anything added onto my bacon before. That experience changed everything. Now I'm a bonafide bacon lover who likes to experiment with new flavor combos at home. This is a sweet and spicy version that really works with the richness of the bacon. There's only a hint of a kick, and we all love it. I serve this not only for breakfast, but as an appetizer or on a dessert table.

Just Peachy Bourbon Spread

Makes 1-1/2 cups

2 (20-ounce) packages
frozen peaches, thawed

2 cups sugar

1 cup bourbon
(see Tip)

Tina's Tip: *Even though the alcohol in the bourbon cooks off, if you'd prefer, you can substitute water, apple juice, or peach nectar for the bourbon.*

1 In a large saucepan over medium-high heat, bring all ingredients to a boil, stirring occasionally.

2 Reduce heat to medium-low and simmer 45 to 60 minutes or until peaches have broken down and liquid has thickened, stirring occasionally.

3 Remove from heat and allow to cool completely. Transfer to an airtight container and chill at least 4 hours before serving.

The only thing better than homemade biscuits or warm-from-the-oven scones is having a fresh and fruity spread to slather them with. This peach spread is great for a spring brunch or a bridal shower. Serve on mini biscuits with baked ham for a tasty appetizer. It's also a wonderful accompaniment to your cheese or charcuterie board.

This perfectly sweet and simple spread can be made a few days ahead, giving you some extra time to work on the rest of your menu. Of course, you can also just make it for the family and keep it in the fridge until someone's looking for something yummy to put on their toast.

Strawberry Shortcake Waffles

Serves 6 to 8

2 cups all-purpose flour

3 tablespoons sugar

1 tablespoon baking powder

½ teaspoon salt

2 eggs, beaten

1-¾ cups milk

¼ cup oil

2 teaspoons vanilla

Sliced fresh strawberries for garnish

Whipped cream for garnish

1 Preheat an electric waffle iron according to directions. Coat with cooking spray.

2 In a large bowl, combine flour, sugar, baking powder, and salt. Stir in eggs, milk, oil, and vanilla; mix well.

3 Using a ½-cup measuring cup (or whatever measure your waffle iron manufacturer recommends), pour batter onto bottom of prepared waffle iron. Close lid and cook 3 to 5 minutes or until golden brown.

4 Using a fork, carefully remove waffle to a plate. Repeat with remaining batter. Top with strawberries and whipped cream.

Tina's Tip: *I like to make a big batch of waffles ... some to eat right away and some to freeze and have on-hand for whenever someone's craving them for breakfast. That way, they can just take one out of the freezer, pop it into the toaster or air fryer, and be on their way. It's so easy and quick!*

Homemade waffles, strawberries, and whipped cream—how could you go wrong? This is such a sweet way to start your day, and it just so happens to be one of my daughter, Lauren's, favorite combinations. When I'm making these for a big family breakfast, I turn the oven on low, place a rack on a baking sheet inside, and set the waffles on the sheet as I finish them. That way, the waffles stay warm and crispy until they're all done and we can all eat together.

PB & B Overnight Oats

Serves 2

1 ripe banana

¼ cup plain Greek yogurt

2 tablespoons peanut butter

1 cup old-fashioned oats

1 teaspoon ground cinnamon

¾ cup milk

1 tablespoon honey

1 teaspoon vanilla

1 In a medium bowl, mash banana. Add remaining ingredients and mix well.

2 Place in mason jars, or plastic containers, so they are portable. Cover and refrigerate overnight. Stir before serving.

Tina's Tip: *These are easy to customize, so if you want to add a few mini chocolate chips, some nuts or seeds, or even other fruit, go for it! Personally, I like to take the chill off the oats by microwaving them for 30 seconds, then stirring in a little more milk.*

We go through a ton of peanut butter and bananas in my house. It's a go-to combination for my girls, who are both on their high school swim team. This recipe is another easy and convenient way for them to enjoy this flavor combo. When I make them, I place them into individual mason jars or Lock & Lock® containers. That way the girls can eat them on their way to their early morning practices or I can enjoy them when I get to QVC.

Chocolate-Almond Crescent Rollups

Makes 16

½ cup (3 ounces) semisweet chocolate chips

1 tablespoon vegetable shortening

1 teaspoon almond or vanilla extract

1 (8-ounce) package refrigerated crescent dinner rolls

2 tablespoons sliced almonds

Powdered sugar for sprinkling

1 Preheat oven to 350 degrees F. In a small saucepan, combine chocolate chips and shortening over low heat, stirring constantly until mixture is melted and smooth. Remove from heat and stir in the extract.

2 Unroll crescent roll dough and separate into 8 triangles. Spread chocolate evenly over each triangle and sprinkle with sliced almonds. Cut each triangle in half lengthwise and roll up, starting at wide end.

3 Place rollups on a rimmed baking sheet and bake 12 to 15 minutes or until golden.

4 Sprinkle with powdered sugar and serve.

Tina's Tip: *Everyone loves pastries for brunch! Set these out next to a coffee station and watch as your guests make them disappear.*

Looking for a quick and delicious breakfast treat? These crescent rollups are so easy to make because they use refrigerated crescent dough—perfect for when you're short on time! Just wait until you pull them out of the oven—each puffy little pastry has plenty of warm gooey chocolate inside and the sliced almonds give them a light crunch that's simply perfect! What a sweet way to start your day!

Lemon-Kissed Raspberry Muffins

Makes 12

2 cups all-purpose flour

¼ teaspoon salt

2 teaspoons baking powder

1 stick butter, softened

1-¼ cups granulated sugar, plus more for sprinkling

2 large eggs

½ cup milk or buttermilk

½ teaspoon vanilla

1 teaspoon lemon juice

1 teaspoon lemon zest

2 cups fresh raspberries

Luscious Lemon Glaze

¾ cup powdered sugar

1 tablespoon lemon juice

½ teaspoon lemon zest

1 teaspoon water

1 Preheat oven to 375 degrees F. Coat a 12-cup muffin tin with cooking spray or use paper liners.

2 In a small bowl, whisk together flour, salt, and baking powder; set aside. In a large bowl with an electric mixer, cream together butter and sugar for several minutes or until fluffy and lighter in color. Add eggs, one at a time, mixing in between. Mix in half the flour mixture, then the milk, vanilla, lemon juice, and lemon zest. Add the rest of the flour mixture and mix until just combined. Fold in the raspberries by hand. Scoop evenly into muffin tin. Sprinkle tops with additional granulated sugar.

3 Bake 22 to 25 minutes or until a toothpick inserted in center comes out clean.

4 Cool in pan 5 minutes, then remove to a wire rack. Meanwhile, to make the Luscious Lemon Glaze, in a small bowl, whisk together powdered sugar, lemon juice, lemon zest, and water. Drizzle on warm muffins.

Tina's Tip: *The buttermilk adds an extra dose of tang and tenderness to these muffins, so if you're choosing between regular milk or buttermilk, I highly recommend the buttermilk!!*

I love all kinds of fruit and finding ways to incorporate them into just about everything. These muffins feature a combo that always reminds me of spring—lemon and berries. (You can swap in blueberries if you prefer.) What you'll get from these muffins is a sweet and tangy taste paired with a soft and moist crumb. They're great for on-the-go or sharing with friends and loved ones.

Tropical Summer Smoothie

Serves 2

1 cup almond milk, coconut water or water

1 tablespoon chia seeds

1 slice crystalized candied ginger

½ orange, peeled

1 ripe banana, cut into chunks

2 cups coarsely chopped kale, stems removed

1 cup frozen pineapple chunks

1 cup frozen mango chunks

1 In a blender, combine all ingredients and blend until smooth, pulsing the blender as needed. Pour into glasses and serve immediately.

For me, this is a great way to get my fruits and veggies in on those days that I'm super busy. I find it so much easier than making and eating a salad when every minute counts. Plus I love how tasty this is.

Strawberry Sunrise Smoothie

Serves 2

2 cups fresh or frozen strawberries, hulled

1-½ cups ice cubes

1 ripe banana, cut into chunks

¼ cup orange juice

½ cup vanilla Greek yogurt

1 tablespoon honey

1 In a blender, combine all ingredients and blend until smooth, pulsing the blender as needed. Pour into glasses and serve immediately.

Lauren has a smoothie for breakfast almost every day. Since she often wakes up before the sun rises, it's an easy way for her to kick-start her morning. The fresh fruit gives her energy, while the Greek yogurt packs in the protein.

Appetizers & Starters

Barbecue Chicken Waffle Sliders 26

Lou's Favorite Thai Chili Wings 28

Bite-Sized Shrimp Egg Rolls 30

Loaded Buffalo Chicken Meatballs 32

Crab Cake Pepper Poppers 34

Cheesy Broccoli "Tots" 35

Southern "Fried" Pickles 36

Spinach-Artichoke Mini Potato Skins 38

Bacon-Wrapped Barbecue Shrimp 40

Cheddar-Bacon Deviled Eggs 42

White Bean Hummus Crostini 43

Quick Pickled Red Onions 44

Cranberry Brie Pull-Apart Bread 46

Street Corn Layer Dip 48

Bee's Knees Blue Cheese Spread 50

Chicken Enchilada Dip 52

Barbecue Chicken Waffle Sliders

Makes 12

24 frozen seasoned waffle fries

12 frozen breaded chicken nuggets

⅓ cup barbecue sauce

24 kosher dill pickle chips

2 slices deli cheddar cheese, each cut into 6 pieces

1 On rimmed baking sheets, heat waffle fries and chicken nuggets according to package directions. Remove from oven, but keep oven on.

2 In a large bowl, toss chicken nuggets with barbecue sauce until evenly coated. Place 2 pickle chips on 12 of the fries, followed by a chicken nugget. Top each with another waffle fry and a piece of cheese. Place baking sheet back into oven for 1 minute or until cheese is melted.

Tina's Tip: *If you want to put these together a few hours before your party, go ahead. Just follow the directions above to assemble them, then when it's party time, simply rewarm them in a 325 degree oven for 10 to 15 minutes.*

We may not catch every game on TV, however we hardly ever miss the big games and love hosting game day parties. And when I do play host, you know there is going to be lots of great food. These sliders are easy to throw together and are popular with everyone. Bring them out on a big platter and dig in!

Lou's Favorite Thai Chili Wings

Serves 4 to 6

1 tablespoon brown sugar

1 teaspoon garlic powder

¾ teaspoon ground ginger

½ teaspoon ground cumin

1 teaspoon salt

½ teaspoon black pepper

4 pounds fresh or frozen chicken wings, thawed

1 tablespoon vegetable oil

⅓ cup Thai chili sauce, heated, plus more for dipping

Thinly sliced scallions for garnish

Tina's Tip: *These can be made in your air fryer too! Just preheat your air fryer to 400 degrees. Add wings, in batches if necessary, and spray with cooking spray. Air fry 13 to 15 minutes, turn them over, and cook another 13 to 15 minutes. Continue with step 5.*

1 Preheat oven to 425 degrees F. Cover a rimmed baking sheet with foil, place a wire rack on the baking sheet, and spray with cooking spray; set aside. (The rack helps the wings get nice and crispy by allowing heat to circulate around them as they cook.)

2 In a small bowl, combine brown sugar, garlic powder, ginger, cumin, salt, and black pepper; mix well.

3 In a large bowl, toss wings with oil. Sprinkle with spice mixture and toss until evenly coated. Place wings in a single layer on prepared rack, making sure they don't touch.

4 Bake 35 minutes, flip wings, and bake 15 to 20 minutes more or until skin is crispy and golden brown, and chicken is cooked through.

5 Place cooked wings in a large bowl, drizzle with Thai chili sauce, and toss until evenly coated. Garnish with scallions.

My husband, Lou, is a big fan of chicken wings. He doesn't really have a preference for flats or drums, but boy does he light up when the wings on his plate are jumbo-sized. Whenever we go to our favorite tavern restaurant, he orders the Thai-flavored wings. Since it isn't always convenient for us to go out to dinner, I came up with a recipe that delivers the same great taste he loves. Now we make these at home whenever we get a craving.

Bite-Sized Shrimp Egg Rolls

Makes 24

¼ cup soy sauce

2 tablespoons brown sugar

½ teaspoon grated fresh ginger
(see Tip)

½ teaspoon minced garlic
(see Tip)

3 cups finely shredded Napa
cabbage

1 small carrot, shredded

2 scallions, chopped

4 ounces frozen cooked salad
shrimp, thawed, drained, and
coarsely chopped

24 wonton wrappers
(not egg roll wrappers)

1 egg, lightly beaten

Cooking spray

Tina's Tip: *Feel free to swap
the fresh ginger and garlic with
a 1 teaspoon each of ground
ginger and garlic powder. And
if you'd like to make a shellfish-
free version, just swap out
the shrimp for a 1/4 pound of
ground pork that's been cooked,
drained, and crumbled.*

1 In a small bowl, combine soy sauce, brown sugar, ginger, and garlic powder; mix well.

2 In a large bowl, combine cabbage, carrot, scallions, and shrimp; mix well. Pour soy sauce mixture over cabbage mixture, toss to coat well, and let stand 10 minutes. Place cabbage mixture in a colander and squeeze to drain well.

3 Preheat oven to 450 degrees F. Coat a rimmed baking sheet with cooking spray.

4 With a corner of the wonton wrappers facing you, spoon about 1 tablespoon cabbage mixture evenly onto center of each wrapper. Lightly brush edges with beaten egg. Fold the corner closest to you over cabbage mixture, then fold both sides in, envelope-style; roll up tightly. Place on baking sheet, seam-side down.

5 Spray a light coating of cooking spray over egg rolls. (This will make them nice and crispy.) Bake 12 to 15 minutes or until golden and crispy. Serve immediately.

I like to serve these with a homemade sweet & sour sauce. To make it, I combine ¾ cup orange marmalade, ½ cup ketchup, 2 tablespoons soy sauce, 2 tablespoons lemon juice, 2 tablespoons light brown sugar, and 1 teaspoon dry mustard in a saucepan over medium-low heat. Cook 3 to 4 minutes or until the sugar is dissolved, stirring often.

Loaded Buffalo Chicken Meatballs

Makes about 25

1 pound ground chicken

1 egg, lightly beaten

¼ cup blue cheese crumbles, plus extra for sprinkling

½ cup breadcrumbs

¼ cup finely chopped celery

1 teaspoon minced fresh garlic

1 teaspoon salt

½ teaspoon black pepper

½ stick butter

⅓ cup cayenne pepper sauce

1 Preheat oven to 400 degrees F. Coat a rimmed baking sheet with cooking spray.

2 In a large bowl, combine chicken, egg, ¼ cup blue cheese, breadcrumbs, celery, garlic, salt, and black pepper; mix until just combined. Form mixture into about 25 meatballs; place on baking sheet. Bake 15 to 18 minutes or until no pink remains in the center of meatballs.

3 Meanwhile, in a large skillet over low heat, melt butter. Stir in cayenne pepper sauce and heat 1 minute. Add meatballs to skillet, tossing until evenly coated. When ready to serve, sprinkle with extra blue cheese crumbles.

Tina's Tip: *To keep these warm, I suggest placing them in a small slow cooker on LOW. Set them alongside some celery sticks with ranch or blue cheese dressing for dipping, and let everyone go to town.*

Buffalo chicken dip is one of those dips that always makes an appearance at any get together. And, who doesn't love a meatball? That's why I came up with a new and different way to incorporate those flavors. These meatballs are always a hit, and because they have blue cheese and the celery mixed in, it's safe to say they are loaded with goodness!

Crab Cake Pepper Poppers

Makes 36

½ cup Italian breadcrumbs

1 egg

¼ cup finely chopped red onion

½ cup finely chopped celery

3 tablespoons mayonnaise

2 teaspoons fresh lemon juice

¾ teaspoon seafood seasoning (like Old Bay®)

¼ teaspoon black pepper

¾ pound fresh lump crabmeat or 2 (6-½-ounce) cans lump crabmeat, drained

18 mini sweet peppers, halved and seeded

Paprika for sprinkling

1 Preheat oven to 350 degrees F. Coat a rimmed baking sheet with cooking spray.

2 In a medium bowl, combine breadcrumbs, egg, onion, celery, mayonnaise, lemon juice, seafood seasoning, and black pepper; mix well. Gently fold in crabmeat, being careful not to break up the chunks.

3 Spoon crabmeat mixture evenly into pepper halves and place on baking sheet.

4 Bake 20 to 25 minutes or until tops are golden and peppers are tender. Sprinkle with paprika before serving.

Tina's Tip: *You can also make these in an air fryer. Simply air fry them 5 to 6 minutes at 350 degrees or until heated through. Depending on the size of your air fryer, you may need to cook them in batches.*

I love crab and since I don't live far from the Chesapeake Bay area, I'm lucky to have an abundance of fresh blue crabs available to me whenever they're in season. So, when life gives you fresh crabs, it's practically your duty to make something tasty, like these mini pepper poppers. (Don't worry, you can also make these with canned crab if you don't have access to fresh crab.)

Cheesy Broccoli "Tots"

Makes about 30

2 (12-ounce) packages frozen broccoli florets, thawed

1 egg

⅓ cup shredded cheddar cheese

⅓ cup plain breadcrumbs

¼ cup minced or finely chopped onion

½ teaspoon garlic powder

¼ teaspoon salt

¼ teaspoon black pepper

Cooking spray

1 Preheat oven to 400 degrees F. Coat rimmed baking sheet(s) with cooking spray.

2 In a blender or food processor with a cutting blade, combine broccoli, egg, cheese, breadcrumbs, onion, garlic powder, salt, and pepper; pulse until mixture is coarsely chopped. (Don't finely chop; you still want some nice texture.)

3 Drop about 30 rounded teaspoonfuls of the mixture onto baking sheet(s). Lightly spray tops with cooking spray. Bake 20 to 25 minutes or until golden brown.

Tina's Tip: *If you are looking for a more "tot-like" shape, you could bake these in mini muffin tins. I like to keep a big batch of these in the freezer. Just freeze them, individually, right on a baking sheet. Once they're frozen, pack them up in a freezer container or bag. When you're ready to reheat some, just place them on a baking sheet in a 325 degree oven for 20 to 25 minutes or until heated through..*

Veggie tots are very popular right now, and you can buy all kinds of frozen varieties at your grocery store. But making these at home allows you to have some fun customizing them, not to mention it's more economical. Forming them to look like traditional tots is a little labor intensive, I prefer a more freeform method. (It doesn't change the taste any!) If you have young kids at home, this is a great way to get them to eat their veggies. They're yummy with ketchup, ranch, or a creamy honey mustard.

Southern "Fried" Pickles

Serves a whole bunch

1 cup yellow cornmeal

½ cup all-purpose flour

1-½ teaspoons dried dill weed

1 teaspoon garlic powder

1 teaspoon salt

¼ teaspoon black pepper

⅛ teaspoon cayenne pepper

¼ cup milk

2 eggs

1 (24-ounce) jar dill pickle chips, drained and patted dry (about 60 slices)

Cooking spray

Ranch dressing for dipping

1 Preheat oven to 425 degrees F. Coat rimmed baking sheet(s) with cooking spray.

2 In a shallow dish, combine cornmeal, flour, dill weed, garlic powder, salt, black pepper, and cayenne pepper; mix well. In another shallow dish, whisk milk and eggs together.

3 Dip pickles into egg mixture, then place in cornmeal mixture to coat evenly. Place on baking sheets. Spray lightly with cooking spray. Bake 15 to 20 minutes or until golden brown.

4 Serve with ranch dressing. (You can use store-bought or better yet, whip up a batch of my Easy Buttermilk Ranch Dressing on page 72.)

Other Cooking Options:

Air Frying: Preheat air fryer to 400 degrees. Coat the basket and pickle chips with cooking spray. Cook in batches, 4 minutes per side.

Deep Frying: In a large pot, heat 3 cups canola oil until hot, but not smoking. Carefully add pickles to oil, in batches, and fry 3 to 4 minutes or until golden, turning once. Drain on a paper towel-lined platter.

Fried pickles are a fun, guilty pleasure. My family loves ordering them as appetizers at some of our favorite bar-style restaurants. These have just the right amount of crunch and a tasty cornmeal coating with just a little bit of spice. With three cooking options to try, you can make them the way you like best.

Spinach-Artichoke Mini Potato Skins

Makes 40

20 small baby red potatoes

1 (8-ounce) package cream cheese, softened

1 (12-ounce) package frozen chopped spinach, thawed and squeezed very dry

1 (13.75-ounce) can artichoke hearts, drained well and chopped

1 cup shredded mozzarella cheese

¼ cup grated Parmesan cheese

½ teaspoon onion powder

½ teaspoon garlic powder

¼ teaspoon salt

¼ teaspoon black pepper

Cooking spray

Tina's Tip: *These can be prepared through step 4 ahead of time, popped in the fridge and then baked right before serving.*

1 Preheat oven to 375 degrees F. Coat a rimmed baking sheet with cooking spray. Place potatoes on baking sheet and pierce all over with a fork.

2 Bake 45 to 50 minutes or until tender. Let stand until cool enough to handle, then cut each potato in half lengthwise. Carefully scoop out the insides of the potatoes, leaving thin shells, and place the skins back on the baking sheet, cut side up. (Save the insides for another use.)

3 In a large bowl with an electric mixer, beat cream cheese until light and fluffy. Add in remaining ingredients, except cooking spray, until combined.

4 Preheat oven to broil. Coat potato skins with cooking spray and broil 4 to 6 minutes or until edges brown.

5 Remove from oven and spoon spinach mixture evenly into skins. Reduce heat to 375 degrees and bake 10 to 15 minutes or until heated through. Serve piping hot.

Spinach-artichoke dip is such a classic, it's hard to find someone who doesn't love it. Rather than serve it up the same old way, I thought it would be a fun idea to put this beloved dip inside creamy, baby red potatoes. It's like a new version of the old-school stuffed potato skin. These are versatile enough to serve at an elegant dinner party or on game day.

Bacon-Wrapped Barbecue Shrimp

Makes about 20

20 wooden toothpicks

10 thick-cut bacon slices

1 pound (about 20) jumbo shrimp, peeled and deveined, tails on

Cracked black pepper for sprinkling

¾ cup barbecue sauce

½ cup apricot preserves

1 Soak wooden toothpicks in water for at least 10 minutes, so they don't burn while they cook.

2 Preheat oven to broil. Coat a rimmed baking sheet with cooking spray. Cut bacon slices in half crosswise. Wrap bacon pieces around shrimp, securing with wooden toothpicks; place on baking sheet. Sprinkle with black pepper.

3 Broil shrimp 3 inches from heat (with oven door partially opened), 4 to 5 minutes per side or until bacon is crisp. (Keep an eye on them, so they don't burn!)

4 Meanwhile, in a small bowl, combine barbecue sauce and apricot preserves; mix well. Reserve ¼ cup for dipping. In a microwave-safe bowl, heat remaining barbecue sauce mixture 1 to 1-½ minutes or until warm.

5 Remove shrimp from oven and brush with warm barbecue sauce mixture. Serve with reserved sauce for dipping.

I love bacon-wrapped shrimp!! With these, the salty smokiness of the bacon complements the sweetness of the sauce. And while I prefer a mustardy-style barbecue sauce, you can go with whatever you like best. These are so delicious, you might want to prepare a double batch!

Cheddar-Bacon Deviled Eggs

Makes 12

6 extra-large eggs

2 tablespoons mayonnaise

1 tablespoon prepared yellow mustard

¼ cup (1 ounce) finely shredded sharp cheddar cheese

⅛ teaspoon salt

½ teaspoon black pepper

2 slices crispy cooked bacon, crumbled

1 avocado, thinly sliced, dipped in lime juice

Tina's Tip: *Unpeeled, hard-boiled eggs can be stored in the refrigerator for up to a week. Once they're peeled, they should be used immediately. The cooking time above is for extra-large eggs, which I suggest using in this recipe because the larger eggs are a little easier to handle. You may need to adjust your cooking time if you use another egg size. (12 minutes for large eggs.)*

1 Place eggs in a large saucepan and add just enough cold water to cover them. Bring to a boil over medium-high heat; remove pan from heat, cover, and let sit 15 minutes.

2 Drain and run cold water over eggs. Add some ice cubes to the water and allow to cool 5 to 10 minutes.

3 Carefully peel eggs and cut in half lengthwise. Remove egg yolks, place in a small bowl, and mash with a fork. Place egg whites on a serving platter.

4 Add mayonnaise, mustard, cheddar cheese, salt, and black pepper to mashed egg yolks; mix well. Fill each egg white half equally with the filling. (You can spoon it on or place the filling inside of a resealable plastic bag and snip off one corner to give your eggs a fancier "piped" look.) Evenly top with crumbled bacon. When ready to serve, garnish with avocado slices.

Deviled eggs make their appearance every year at our Easter celebration, thanks to my sister, Nancy. She usually makes one big batch of eggs and changes up the filling. They're so versatile, you can easily customize them to your taste preferences, whether you like a little hot sauce or a certain type of mustard—like horseradish, honey, or Dijon. This version reminds me of an egg-topped avocado toast (like the one on page 8), but with the addition of crispy bacon.

White Bean Hummus Crostini

Makes 24

White Bean Hummus

2 small cloves garlic, peeled

1 (15-ounce) can cannellini beans, rinsed and drained

¼ cup tahini (see Tip)

¼ cup lemon juice

1-½ teaspoons ground cumin

1 sprig fresh rosemary, stem removed

½ teaspoon salt

1 French baguette

Olive oil for drizzling

Salt and pepper for sprinkling

1 cup arugula

Pickled red onions (see recipe on page 44)

1 Preheat oven to 450 degrees F.

2 To make the White Bean Hummus, in a food processor, process garlic until minced. Add cannellini beans, tahini, lemon juice, cumin, rosemary, and salt. Process until mixture is smooth, scraping down sides of bowl as needed. Set aside to allow the flavors to "marry."

3 Slice the baguette diagonally into 24 (½-inch-thick) slices and arrange on a rimmed baking sheet. Drizzle with olive oil, sprinkle with salt and pepper, and toast 6 to 8 minutes or until golden.

4 Spread hummus on each crostini, evenly top with arugula and pickled onions, and enjoy.

Tina's Tip: *Not sure what tahini is or where to find it? It's simply a paste made from ground sesame seeds, which has the consistency of thin peanut butter. It's typically found in the ethnic section of most grocery stores.*

This is a recipe that delivers a variety of textures and flavors. You have the creamy and hearty cannellini beans with the flavorful and aromatic fresh rosemary. Then there's the tart pickled onions and the peppery arugula on top of the crusty baguette. It's just perfection. You can serve these assembled or create a grazing board by placing your hummus in a serving dish and surround it with all the toppings. It's like a crostini bar, where your guests can make their own!

Quick Pickled Red Onions

Makes 2 cups

1 large red onion, thinly sliced

3 sprigs fresh thyme

1-½ cups red wine vinegar

2-½ tablespoons sugar

1 tablespoon salt

1 tablespoon black peppercorns

1 Add onion and thyme sprigs to heat-safe jar(s).

2 In a medium saucepan over medium heat, combine vinegar, sugar, salt, and peppercorns. Bring to a boil, stirring to make sure sugar is dissolved. Turn off heat and let cool about 10 minutes.

3 Pour liquid over onions in jar(s). Cover and refrigerate for up to two weeks.

Tina's Tips: *If you want to kick up the flavor, add a shake or two of red pepper flakes. These also make cute hostess gifts! Just place them into a nice jar, tie a pretty ribbon around it, and you're all set!*

I will admit it—I don't really like raw onions. When I order a salad, I tend to ask them to leave out the raw onions; otherwise, I feel like I'm tasting them all day. But *pickling* onions changes everything. I think it takes out some of their bite or "rawness" and makes them really tasty. They are so good on just about anything—pizza, tacos, hamburgers, hot dogs...you name it!

Cranberry Brie Pull-Apart Bread

Serves 8 to 10

1 pound round sourdough bread, unsliced

1 (15-ounce) can whole-berry cranberry sauce

1 (8-ounce) wheel of Brie, cut into thin strips

2 teaspoons fresh thyme leaves

Tina's Tip: *Going over to a friend's house for the holidays? This is a great appetizer to bring along. Just wrap it up in the foil and bake it when you're ready to serve it.*

1 Preheat oven to 375 degrees F. Tear a piece of aluminum foil large enough to loosely wrap the whole bread.

2 Using a serrated knife, make a series of parallel cuts in bread about 1-inch apart and about 2-inches deep. Then rotate bread and cut in the opposite direction until you end up with a crisscross pattern (see photo). Place bread on foil.

3 Evenly spoon cranberry sauce between cuts of bread, being careful not to break bread apart. Stuff strips of brie between each bread section. Sprinkle with fresh thyme leaves. Wrap bread loosely in foil.

4 Place foil-wrapped loaf on a baking sheet and bake 30 minutes or until bread is crispy on top and bottom, and Brie is melty.

A fun twist on the typical baked Brie. This is an appetizer that's great for the holidays, especially because it calls for cranberry sauce. I use canned cranberry sauce as a shortcut here, since I typically make a fresh cranberry relish to serve with dinner. We're all busy at holiday time, so a few shortcuts can help to make the busy holiday season more enjoyable and delicious!

Street Corn Layer Dip

Serves 8 to 10

1 (8-ounce) package cream cheese, softened

1 cup sour cream

1 (1-ounce) packet taco seasoning

1 cup black beans, drained and rinsed

1 cup frozen corn, thawed (see Tip)

1 cup diced tomatoes

¼ cup sliced black olives

1 avocado, halved, pitted, diced, and tossed with lime juice

2 tablespoons grated cotija cheese

Tortilla chips for serving

1 In a large bowl with an electric mixer, beat cream cheese until light and fluffy, and no lumps remain. Add sour cream and taco seasoning; mix until combined.

2 Spread mixture onto a rimmed serving platter. Layer with beans, corn, tomatoes, olives, and avocado; sprinkle with cotija cheese.

3 Cover with plastic wrap and refrigerate until ready to serve. Serve with tortilla chips for dipping.

Tina's Tip: *You can always use fresh corn when it's in season. Just roast them in their husks, by placing them directly on your oven rack at 400 degrees for 30 to 35 minutes or until tender.*

The beauty of a dip like this is that it's totally customizable. Everyone has their favorite way of making a Mexican layered dip—for some that means leaving out the olives or swapping out the cotija cheese for feta cheese. This is the way my family enjoys this dip. Lots of times, when I make corn on the cob, I make a little extra so I have corn on standby for this recipe (or to add to a salad).

Bee's Knees Blue Cheese Spread

Makes 1-1/2 cups

1 (8-ounce) package cream cheese, softened

⅓ cup blue cheese crumbles

¼ cup pecans, chopped, plus extra for garnish

1 scallion, thinly sliced, plus extra for garnish

2 strips crispy cooked bacon, crumbled, plus extra for garnish

2 tablespoons honey, plus extra for drizzling

Soft pretzel nuggets or crackers for serving

1 Preheat oven to 350 degrees F.

2 In a medium bowl, combine cream cheese, blue cheese, pecans, scallion, bacon, and honey. Spoon into a 1-quart baking dish.

3 Bake 25 to 30 minutes or until heated through and golden.

4 Garnish with extra pecans, scallion, and bacon, drizzle with more honey, and serve with pretzel nuggets or crackers.

Tina's Tip: *I buy about 10 pounds of honey from my sister-in-law every year. I keep a couple pounds for myself, then give the rest away as gifts. To make the gifts even sweeter, you can attach a tag with the recipe for this spread on each jar. Some ribbon and a handmade label and you're golden!*

Because I write a food blog, (epicuricloud.com) I wanted to learn more about the whole process of harvesting honey. Fortunately for me, my sister-in-law, Laura, is a beekeeper. Years ago, my girls and I got to spend an afternoon checking out the hive and harvesting the honey. It was such a great experience—if you have the opportunity to learn more about bees and honey, I recommend it. Without honey, this spread wouldn't taste as sweet as it does!

Chicken Enchilada Dip

Serves 14 to 16

1 (8-ounce) package cream cheese, softened

2 tablespoons taco seasoning

Juice of half a lime

1 (4-ounce) can diced green chiles

1 (19-ounce) can red enchilada sauce

½ cup frozen corn, thawed

2 cups shredded cooked chicken (see Tip)

3 cups shredded colby jack cheese, divided

Tortilla chips (optional)

Sliced jalapeños (optional)

Fresh cilantro (optional)

1 Preheat oven to 350 degrees F.

2 In a large bowl, with an electric mixer, beat together cream cheese, taco seasoning, and lime juice. Then stir in chiles, enchilada sauce, and corn. Fold in shredded chicken and 2 cups shredded cheese; mix well.

3 Spread mixture in a 2-quart baking dish and top with remaining 1 cup shredded cheese.

4 Bake 25 to 30 minutes or until bubbly. Serve with tortilla chips, jalapeños, and cilantro, if desired.

Tina's Tip: *An easy way to shred or "pull" chicken is to place warm, moist cooked chicken in a bowl. Then use your hand mixer (with traditional beaters) or stand mixer (with flat beater) and mix on medium speed until you get your desired amount of shred.*

You might have seen me make a version of this on QVC in a slow cooker. (It's a favorite on the set.) Say hello to the oven version! This dip is for anyone who loves chicken enchiladas, but is looking for an easier way to get all the flavors without actually preparing chicken enchiladas. You can use cooked leftover chicken from the night before or start with a store-bought rotisserie chicken.

Soups, Salads, & Sandwiches

Slow Cooker Chili Soup 56

Creamy Broccoli & Cheddar Soup 58

Chunky Chicken Noodle Soup 60

Simple Lentil Soup 61

"Stuffed Mushroom" Florentine Soup 62

Busy Weeknight Tortilla Soup 64

Grilled Steak Mediterranean Salad 65

Chicken Salad Lettuce Wraps 66

Salmon Caesar Salad 68

Farmer's Market Spinach Salad 69

Italian-Style Quinoa Bowls 70

Easy Buttermilk Ranch Dressing 72

Crispy Crunchy Croutons 72

Taste of Tuscany Grilled Cheese 73

Cheesy Chicken & Pimiento Melts 74

Egg Salad BLT Sandwiches 76

Open-Faced Portobello "Steak" Sandwiches 77

My Mom's Super Sandwiches 78

Slow Cooker Chili Soup

Serves 6 to 8

1-½ pounds ground beef

1 onion chopped

2 (14-½-ounce) cans diced tomatoes, undrained

1 clove garlic, chopped

1-½ cups water

2 (16-ounce) cans kidney beans, undrained

1-½ cups frozen corn

1 (16-ounce) can tomato sauce

1 tablespoon chili powder

1 teaspoon ground cumin

½ teaspoon salt

1 In a large skillet over medium-high heat, sauté ground beef and onion 5 to 7 minutes or until browned; drain excess fat.

2 Place beef mixture into a 4-quart or larger slow cooker. Add remaining ingredients; mix well.

3 Cover and cook on HIGH 3 to 4 hours or LOW 6 to 7 hours.

Tina's Tip: *My family loves when I set out an assortment of toppings. That way, they can add their own special touches. I like topping my bowl with a dollop of sour cream, avocado, a bit of cilantro, and a squeeze of lime juice.*

SOUPS, SALADS & SANDWICHES

Rich and flavorful soups and chili are some of my favorite dishes to make. They are warm, comforting, and everyone loves to settle in with a big bowl. I'm a big fan of chili as it sort of runs in my blood. Both sides of my family are from Cincinnati. While I do often make my own version of Cincinnati chili (over spaghetti) I really love all types of chili and soup. With this chili soup recipe, you get the best of both worlds. Plus, it's made in a slow cooker, so it's really easy!

Creamy Broccoli & Cheddar Soup

Serves 4 to 6

5 cups chicken broth

1 head broccoli, trimmed and coarsely chopped

½ cup grated carrots

½ teaspoon black pepper

6 tablespoons butter

¼ cup finely chopped onion

½ cup all-purpose flour

1 cup heavy cream (see Tip)

⅛ teaspoon nutmeg (optional)

3 cups (12 ounces) shredded cheddar cheese

Salt to taste

1 In a soup pot over high heat, combine chicken broth, broccoli, carrots, and pepper; bring to a boil. Reduce heat to low, cover, and simmer 10 minutes or until broccoli is tender.

2 Meanwhile, in a skillet over medium heat, heat butter until melted. Add onion and sauté until softened. Stir in flour and let cook 1 to 2 minutes or until it starts to turn golden. Slowly whisk about 1-¼ cups of the hot broth into the butter-flour mixture (roux) until well blended, stirring continuously.

3 Gradually add onion roux to soup, stirring until thickened; simmer 5 minutes. Slowly stir in heavy cream and nutmeg, if desired. Add cheese, 1 cup at a time, stirring after each addition, until cheese is melted. Add salt to taste and serve hot.

Tina's Tip: *To lighten this up, you can substitute equal amounts of whole milk or half & half in place of the heavy cream.*

My girls love the cream of broccoli cheddar soup at Panera Bread®, which is all the inspiration I needed to try and recreate it at home. After some tweaking and testing, I finally got it just right. My girls not only approve of my version, but actually admit they like it even more. Now that's what I call a #momwin!

Chunky Chicken Noodle Soup

Serves 8 to 10

2 tablespoons vegetable oil

3 carrots, cut into ½-inch chunks

2 stalks celery, cut into ½-inch chunks

1 onion, cut into ½-inch chunks

2 medium cloves garlic, chopped

1 (3-½ to 4 pound) chicken, cut into 8 pieces

8 cups cold water

1 (32-ounce) container chicken broth (regular or low sodium)

3 sprigs fresh thyme

1 bay leaf

1 teaspoon salt

½ teaspoon black pepper

1 tablespoon chopped fresh parsley

8 ounces egg noodles, cooked according to package directions

1 In a soup pot over medium heat, heat oil until hot; sauté carrots, celery, onion, and garlic 5 to 7 minutes or until vegetables begin to soften. Add chicken, water, chicken broth, thyme, bay leaf, salt, and pepper; bring to a boil. Reduce heat to low and simmer 1 hour or until chicken falls off the bones.

2 Using tongs, carefully remove chicken, thyme, and bay leaf from soup; allow chicken to cool slightly. Remove chicken meat, discarding bones and skin.

3 Pull chicken into bite-sized pieces and return to soup. Right before you're ready to serve, stir in parsley and cooked noodles, and simmer until heated through.

This is one of my all-time favorite soups. As a kid I would add crumbled saltine crackers to make it even heartier. These days, I always keep a few containers of soup in my freezer, so if and when someone in the family gets the sniffles, I'm ready with a steaming bowl. Just remember, if you want to freeze it like I do, don't add the noodles until just before you serve it.

Simple Lentil Soup

Serves 5 to 6

2 tablespoons olive oil

1 onion, chopped

3 medium cloves garlic, minced

3 cups water

5 cups beef broth
(regular or low sodium)

1 (12-ounce) package dried
lentils, washed and drained

3 carrots, finely chopped

1 bay leaf

½ teaspoon salt,
plus more to taste

½ teaspoon black pepper

1 In a soup pot over medium heat, heat oil until hot; sauté onion and garlic 3 minutes or until tender. Add remaining ingredients; bring to a boil over medium-high heat.

2 Reduce heat to low, cover, and simmer 50 to 60 minutes, stirring occasionally or until lentils are tender, stirring occasionally. Discard bay leaf before serving. Add additional salt to taste.

Tina's Tip: *Lentils come in a rainbow of colors—green, red, yellow, and black to name a few. Feel free to mix and match, or use whichever one you have in your pantry.*

Lentils are getting a lot of attention these days, and for good reason. For starters, they are a great source of protein and fiber. They're also low-fat and full of nutrients, like iron and calcium. In my house, we eat lentils pretty frequently, either in the form of simple soups like this, over some rice or veggies, or even for breakfast. (I make a morning protein bar that's loaded with lentils!)

"Stuffed Mushroom" Florentine Soup

Serves 4 to 5

1-½ pounds cremini (baby bella) mushrooms, stems trimmed

4 tablespoons olive oil, divided

¼ teaspoon salt

½ teaspoon black pepper

½ teaspoon fresh thyme leaves

1 teaspoon minced garlic

2 tablespoons dry Marsala wine

6 cups (48 ounces) chicken broth (regular or low sodium)

½ pound sweet Italian sausage, casing removed

¼ cup panko breadcrumbs

1 tablespoon grated Parmesan cheese, plus extra for topping

1 cup loosely packed baby spinach (stems removed)

1 Wipe mushrooms with a damp paper towel to clean; thinly slice. Remove ½ cup of sliced mushrooms and set aside.

2 In a large pot over medium heat, add 2 tablespoons olive oil, remaining sliced mushrooms, salt, and pepper; sauté 5 minutes or until tender. Add thyme and garlic, and sauté 30 seconds, just long enough for the thyme and garlic to become fragrant. Add wine and stir to deglaze pan. Stir in chicken broth, bring to a boil, then reduce heat to simmer; cover and cook 15 minutes.

3 Meanwhile, to make sausage meatballs, finely chop reserved ½ cup of mushrooms. In a medium bowl, add sausage, minced mushrooms, breadcrumbs, and 1 tablespoon Parmesan cheese; mix well. Roll to form about 16 (1-inch) meatballs. In a large skillet over medium heat, heat remaining 2 tablespoons olive oil until hot. Add meatballs and brown on all sides about 10 minutes or until cooked through.

4 Add spinach and cooked meatballs to soup. Stir and continue to cook until spinach is wilted. Dish up and top each bowl with Parmesan cheese, as desired.

This soup actually brought me to tears. It all happened when I won first place in the Kennett Square Mushroom Soup Contest. (Kennett Square, in Pennsylvania, is known as the "Mushroom Capital of the World," and every year they hold a huge festival.) This was the first contest where I won first place, so when I did, I cried. After all the fanfare, my entire family went over to a booth where we each got big scoops of ice cream. I was the only one who chose the special cream of mushroom flavor!

Busy Weeknight Tortilla Soup

Serves 8 to 10

7 cups chicken broth (regular or low sodium)

1 cup water

1 (16-ounce) jar medium salsa

1 cup frozen corn, thawed

1 pound boneless, skinless chicken breasts, cut into ½-inch chunks

4 (6-inch) flour tortillas, cut into ¼- x 3-inch strips

Finely shredded cheddar cheese for sprinkling

1 In a soup pot over high heat, bring chicken broth, water, and salsa to a boil.

2 Add corn and chicken, and cook 4 to 6 minutes or until no pink remains.

3 Right before serving, stir in tortilla strips and cook 2 to 3 minutes or until heated through. Sprinkle each bowl with cheese and enjoy.

Tina's Tip: *Take your tortilla soup to the next level with toppings. I suggest chunks of avocado, sliced jalapeños, and sour cream.*

As much as I love to cook, there are days where I'm just too busy to go all out for dinner. Fortunately, I have a number of really easy, throw-together recipes that my family loves. Don't let the simplicity of this soup fool you. The salsa adds lots of flavor while the tortillas turn into South-of-the-Border-style noodles.

Grilled Steak Mediterranean Salad

Serves 4 to 6

¼ cup olive oil

Juice of 1 lemon

1 small onion, finely chopped

1 teaspoon minced garlic

2 teaspoons crushed red pepper

1 teaspoon salt

1 (1-½-pound) beef flank steak

1 head romaine lettuce, cut into bite-sized pieces

⅓ cup pitted Kalamata olives

1 (4-ounce) package crumbled feta cheese

1 cup grape tomatoes, halved

¾ cup Greek dressing (see Tip)

1 In a large resealable plastic bag, combine olive oil, lemon juice, onion, garlic, crushed red pepper, and salt; mix well. Add steak, seal bag, and shake gently to completely coat steak. Chill 4 hours or overnight, turning halfway through the marinating time.

2 Place lettuce on a serving platter; set aside. Remove steak from marinade, discarding any excess marinade, and place on a grill or grill pan over high heat. Grill 5 to 6 minutes per side for medium or until desired doneness. Remove steak to a cutting board and let rest 5 minutes before slicing across the grain.

3 Arrange steak slices over lettuce and top with olives, feta cheese, and tomatoes. Drizzle with Greek dressing.

Tina's Tip: *You can use a store-bought dressing if you'd like, but for a taste of the Greek Islands, make your own by combining 3/4 cup olive oil, 1/3 cup fresh lemon juice, 1 tablespoon dried oregano, 1/2 teaspoon finely chopped garlic, 1/2 teaspoon salt, and 1/4 teaspoon black pepper in a jar with a tight-fitting lid. After putting on the lid, just give it a good shake until it's well combined.*

Not only do I like making big salads—the kind where everyone can serve themselves—but I'm also a year-round griller. You should see me out there in the middle of winter, shoveling my deck with my parka on, just so I can get to the grill! No matter the weather, this salad will bring a taste of the Mediterranean to your table. And if you're lighting up the grill to make this, why not grill some crusty bread to serve with it?

Chicken Salad Lettuce Wraps

Makes 8

1 pound cooked chicken breasts, cut into 1-inch pieces

½ cup pecan pieces

1 stalk celery, chopped

1 cup red seedless grapes, cut in half

Honey-Yogurt Dressing

3 tablespoons plain Greek yogurt (see Tip)

3 tablespoons mayonnaise

1 tablespoon honey

1 tablespoon finely chopped red onion

½ teaspoon salt

¼ teaspoon black pepper

8 romaine or bibb lettuce leaves

1 In a large bowl, combine chicken, pecans, celery, and grapes.

2 To make the Honey-Yogurt Dressing, in a small bowl, combine yogurt, mayonnaise, honey, onion, salt, and pepper; whisk to combine. Toss chicken mixture with dressing until well coated.

3 Spoon chicken salad evenly onto each lettuce leaf and enjoy.

Tina's Tip: *Make sure you use plain, unflavored Greek yogurt (not vanilla) or you'll end up with a dressing that's too sweet. I like to use Greek yogurt because it adds extra protein and has a thicker consistency.*

These are a lighter take on a traditional chicken salad sandwich. An easy swap from buns to lettuce leaves makes these a great low-carb option. Every bite features plenty of crunch (thanks to the pecans and celery), and the combination of grapes with my homemade Honey-Yogurt Dressing adds the perfect amount of sweetness. Make these for lunch or serve them at a spring brunch or shower.

Salmon Caesar Salad

Serves 4

4 salmon fillets (about 1 pound total)

1 (1.2-ounce) envelope Caesar salad dressing mix, divided

½ cup olive oil

¼ cup white vinegar

1 (2-ounce) can anchovies, drained and finely chopped (optional)

1 large head romaine lettuce, cut into bite-sized pieces

¼ cup grated Parmesan cheese

1 (6-ounce) package croutons (see Tip)

1 Preheat the broiler. Coat a broiler pan with cooking spray.

2 Place salmon on broiler pan and rub top of each fillet with 1 teaspoon of dry dressing mix.

3 Broil 6 to 8 minutes or until top is golden, and it flakes easily with a fork. (Your cooking time will vary based on the thickness of your fillets.)

4 In a large bowl, combine oil, vinegar, anchovies, if desired, and the remaining dressing mix; mix well. Add lettuce, Parmesan cheese, and croutons, and toss until thoroughly coated. Divide mixture evenly onto 4 salad plates and top each with a salmon fillet. Serve immediately.

Tina's Tip: *Everyone in my family loves the crunchy texture that croutons add to a salad. If you'd like to try your hand at making your own, check out my recipe for them on page 72.*

Okay, I'll admit it—I do not really care for many salmon dishes. However, I know that many of you do, so this one is just for you. It's a classic Caesar salad topped with a perfectly cooked and seasoned salmon fillet. I hope you'll let me know how I did on this one. I know my taste testers gave it two thumbs up (and if you're like me and do not care for salmon, you can still enjoy this salad fish-free!).

Farmer's Market Spinach Salad

Serves 4 to 6

12 ounces fresh baby spinach

1 pint fresh strawberries, washed, hulled, and sliced

2 oranges, peeled and cut into segments (see Tip)

1 cup Italian dressing (see Tip)

1 to 2 tablespoons finely minced red onion

¼ cup granulated sugar

½ cup crumbled blue cheese

1 In a large salad bowl, combine spinach, strawberries, and oranges.

2 In a small bowl, combine Italian dressing, onion, and sugar; mix well.

3 Sprinkle salad with blue cheese and serve with dressing. Refrigerate any leftover dressing for up to 2 weeks.

Tina's Tip: *If you don't feel like peeling a fresh orange, use a can of mandarin oranges that you've drained. Plus, if you want to make your own dressing instead of buying it, the Red Wine Vinaigrette on page 70 would be delicious with this recipe.*

I love a fresh and colorful salad, especially one that you can change with the seasons. The fruit in this salad can be swapped out depending on what's fresh at the market. While I suggest starting with strawberries and oranges, you can definitely substitute with blueberries or raspberries in the late summer months or use diced pear instead of oranges when fall rolls around. Use what's in season and make it your own—it's hard to go wrong!

Italian-Style Quinoa Bowls

Serves 4 to 6

1 cup uncooked quinoa

Red Wine Vinaigrette

½ cup olive oil

3 tablespoons red wine vinegar

1 teaspoon fresh minced garlic

2 teaspoons Dijon mustard

1 teaspoon Italian seasoning

1 teaspoon salt

¼ teaspoon black pepper

1-½ cups grape tomatoes, cut in half

1 cup seeded and diced cucumber

2 tablespoons chopped red onion

1 (7.75-ounce) can chickpeas, rinsed and drained

1 (14-ounce) can quartered artichoke hearts, drained

1 cup mini fresh mozzarella balls

¼ cup fresh basil, slivered

1 Cook quinoa according to package directions. Place in a bowl and set aside to cool.

2 Meanwhile, to make the Red Wine Vinaigrette, in a small bowl, whisk together all ingredients. Drizzle over quinoa and toss until evenly coated.

3 Set out tomatoes, cucumber, onion, chickpeas, artichokes, mozzarella balls, and basil in bowls, along with the quinoa, and let everyone create their own customized bowl.

Tina's Tip: *For making quick sauces and dressings, I love to use my KitchenAid® Chopper. It can chop up the garlic and emulsify the oil and vinegar in seconds.*

Between my busy QVC schedule and the girls' busy athletic, school, and work schedules, we're on the go a lot. These grain bowls make the perfect lunch or a light dinner. What works best for my family is to set out a bunch of toppings—you know, cut-up tomatoes, cukes, and mozzarella balls—and everyone can customize their own bowl. Sometimes I even put out some chopped, grilled chicken or steak so they can add that too if they want heartier bowls. Whether they eat these at home or pack them in individual containers to-go, everyone's happy. (I love my Lock & Lock® containers!)

Easy Buttermilk Ranch Dressing

Makes 1-1/2 cups

1 cup mayonnaise

½ cup buttermilk

2 tablespoons pickle juice (from a jar of pickles)

½ teaspoon onion powder

½ teaspoon garlic powder

½ teaspoon dill weed

½ teaspoon celery salt

½ teaspoon salt

½ teaspoon black pepper

2 tablespoons fresh minced parsley

1 Place all ingredients in a jar with a tight-fitting lid and shake until well combined, or place in a small food processor or chopper and pulse until creamy smooth. Refrigerate until ready to use.

Make your own delicious and creamy dressing to top your favorite salads with. This one is also great for dipping things like my Cheesy Broccoli "Tots" or my Southern "Fried" Pickles. (See pages 35 and 36.)

Crispy Crunchy Croutons

Makes 4 cups

½ stick butter, melted

½ teaspoon garlic powder

½ teaspoon salt

⅛ teaspoon black pepper

½ loaf French bread, cut into 1-inch cubes

1 Preheat oven to 375 degrees F. In a small bowl, combine butter, garlic powder, salt, and pepper. Place bread cubes in a large bowl and toss with butter mixture.

2 Place coated bread cubes onto a rimmed baking sheet and bake 15 to 20 minutes or until crispy and golden, stirring halfway through cooking. Let cool and store in an airtight container until ready to use.

Add a little crunch to your salads with my easy homemade croutons. They're buttery and lightly seasoned, so they pair perfectly with just about any kind of salad.

Taste of Tuscany Grilled Cheese

Makes 4

¼ cup prepared pesto sauce (see Tip)

4 ciabatta rolls, split in half

1 cup roasted red peppers, patted dry

1 (8-ounce) ball fresh mozzarella, cut into 8 slices and patted dry

½ cup fresh basil leaves

Black pepper for sprinkling

¼ cup olive oil

1 Evenly spread pesto on the cut side of the bottom half of each roll. Top each with roasted peppers, 2 slices mozzarella cheese, basil, and a sprinkle of black pepper. Place tops of rolls back on and brush both sides of sandwiches with olive oil.

2 In a grill pan or skillet over medium-low heat, grill sandwiches until golden brown on both sides and cheese begins to melt. To make these more panini-style, place a heavy pan on top of sandwiches and press down as they cook.

Tina's Tip: *To avoid a watery sandwich, make sure to pat the roasted peppers and each slice of mozzarella cheese with a paper towel before building your sandwich. And if you want to make your own homemade pesto, see page 150.*

We love grilled cheese and panini sandwiches at our house. This recipe is a delicious combination of both. Paired with some soup or salad, this makes a tasty lunch or a light supper.

Cheesy Chicken & Pimiento Melts

Makes 4

1 (8-ounce) package cream cheese, softened

½ cup mayonnaise

1 (4-ounce) jar chopped pimientos, drained well

½ teaspoon onion powder

½ teaspoon garlic powder

½ teaspoon paprika

½ teaspoon black pepper

1 teaspoon hot sauce (or more, depending on how much spice you like)

2 cups (8 ounces) finely shredded sharp cheddar cheese

1 cup shredded rotisserie chicken

8 slices country-style bread

½ stick butter, softened

1 In a medium bowl with an electric mixer, beat cream cheese until smooth. Add mayonnaise, pimientos, onion and garlic powders, paprika, pepper, and hot sauce; mix until combined. Mix in cheese and chicken until well blended.

2 Spread 4 slices of bread evenly with mixture. Top with remaining slices of bread. Spread butter on both sides of sandwiches.

3 In a skillet or on a griddle over medium heat, cook in batches until both sides are golden and cheese is melty.

If you thought you were only getting one grilled cheese sandwich in this book, you're in for a treat. This is a more Southern-inspired version of that melty-good sandwich. The homemade pimiento cheese spread is creamy and gooey, and best served between thick slices of country-style bread. I may not be a Southern girl, but I think I've done this sandwich justice. Of course, I'll let you be the judge.

Egg Salad BLT Sandwiches

Makes 4

8 hard-boiled eggs (see Tip)

3 tablespoons mayonnaise

¼ teaspoon salt

⅛ teaspoon black pepper

4 strips cooked bacon, chopped

1 tomato, seeded and diced

8 slices hearty white or whole-wheat bread

4 butter or bibb lettuce leaves

1 In a large bowl, coarsely chop eggs. Stir in mayonnaise, salt, pepper, bacon, and tomato; mix well.

2 Meanwhile, toast bread.

3 Spread egg mixture evenly over 4 slices of bread, then top with lettuce and remaining bread. Serve immediately.

Tina's Tip: *To make the perfect hard-boiled eggs, place them in a medium saucepan and cover with water. Over medium-high heat, bring to a boil. Once boiling, remove from heat, cover the pan and let sit, 12 minutes for large eggs and 15 minutes for extra-large. Drain and add cold, iced water to the pan and let sit 3 minutes before peeling.*

"Two classics. One sandwich. A fantastic mash-up." That's the tagline for these yummy sandwiches. Toasted bread and crispy bacon make them perfect. These are great after Easter, when you have more hard-boiled eggs than you know what to do with them.

Open-Faced Portobello "Steak" Sandwiches

Serves 6 to 8

3 tablespoons butter

3 tablespoons olive oil

3 onions, thinly sliced

1-¼ pounds (about 5 to 6) portobello mushrooms, stems on, cut into ⅛-inch-thick slices

¼ cup bottled steak sauce

1 loaf French bread, cut in half lengthwise

8 ounces sliced provolone cheese

1 In a large skillet over medium-high heat, heat butter and oil until butter is melted. Sauté onions 8 to 10 minutes or until golden. Remove to a bowl.

2 Meanwhile, preheat oven to 400 degrees F. Add mushrooms to skillet, reduce heat to medium, and cook 3 to 5 minutes or until tender. Return onions to skillet, add steak sauce, and toss until everything is well combined.

3 Divide mushroom mixture evenly over bread halves, top with cheese, and place on a rimmed baking sheet.

4 Bake on upper rack in oven 5 to 6 minutes or until cheese is melted and top begins to turn golden. Using a serrated knife, cut diagonally into 6 to 8 pieces and enjoy.

A lot of people are practicing meatless Mondays now, which I think is a pretty neat idea. There are so many delicious dinner ideas that are plant-based, like these open-faced, Philly cheesesteak-inspired sandwiches. Portobello mushrooms are hearty and thick, and when you season them just right, they deliver the same kind of flavors you'd expect from a classic Philly cheesesteak.

My Mom's Super Sandwiches

Makes 4

6 tablespoons butter

2 tablespoons minced onion

1-½ teaspoons poppy seeds

2 tablespoons yellow mustard

4 hamburger buns, sliced

½ pound thinly sliced deli ham

4 slices Swiss cheese

1 Preheat oven to 350 degrees F.

2 In a small saucepan over low heat, melt butter with onion, poppy seeds, and mustard for 3 to 5 minutes or until onion is softened.

3 Spread butter mixture on inside of buns; top with ham and cheese. Loosely wrap each sandwich in aluminum foil and place on baking sheet.

4 Heat 15 to 18 minutes or until toasty hot and cheese is melted.

Tina's Tip: *These are great to make in advance and heat at the last minute, which makes them perfect for any occasion when company is coming over.*

Growing up, my mom would make a whole bunch of these. They were great for big gatherings (which every gathering inevitably was, since just our family made up 8!). We called them "Super Sandwiches." Later on in life, my friend, Gail, would bring a slider version of them to our Christmas Eve "Feast of Seven Appetizers." She called them "Ham Biscuits." The way I see it, no matter what you call them, they're a family favorite.

Chicken & Turkey

One-Pan Parmesan Chicken 82

Slow Cooker Balsamic Chicken 84

Sheet Pan Chicken Supper 86

Weeknight-Friendly Chicken Cacciatore 87

Dill-icious Oven-Fried Chicken 88

Pennsylvania Dutch Chicken & Dumplings 90

Bundt Pan Roasted Chicken 91

Cornbread Taco Casserole 92

Coconut Curry Chicken Skewers 94

Skillet Chicken & White Wine Mushrooms 95

Maui BBQ Chicken 96

Simmering Greek Chicken 98

Italian-Stuffed Chicken Cutlets 99

Parmesan Turkey Patties 100

Herb-Brined Roasted Turkey 102

Flavorful Turkey Brine 103

One-Pan Parmesan Chicken

Serves 4

4 boneless skinless chicken breasts

½ teaspoon salt

¼ teaspoon black pepper

2 tablespoons olive oil

½ cup chopped onion

1 cup diced red bell pepper

1 medium clove garlic, minced

1 teaspoon Italian seasoning

½ cup chicken broth (regular or low sodium)

½ cup heavy cream

¾ cup grated Parmesan cheese, divided

1 cup fresh baby spinach, sliced

1 Sprinkle chicken breasts evenly with salt and pepper. In a large skillet over medium heat, heat oil until hot. Brown chicken about 4 minutes on each side, then remove to a plate and cover to keep warm.

2 To the same skillet, add onion, red bell pepper, garlic, and Italian seasoning. Cook about 2 minutes, stirring occasionally. Add chicken broth and scrape up any bits from the bottom of the pan. Add cream and bring to a simmer. Add ½ cup Parmesan cheese; stir about 2 minutes or until cheese melts and sauce begins to thicken.

3 Add chicken breasts back to pan. Cover, reduce heat to low, and simmer 5 to 6 minutes or until chicken is cooked through and internal temperature reaches 165 degrees. Sprinkle with spinach and remaining ¼ cup Parmesan cheese and serve.

This creamy chicken is one of my all-time favorites. It is an easy one-pan dish that my family absolutely loves. Not only is it weeknight-friendly, but it's super saucy, super flavorful, and just plain delicious. I usually serve it alongside one of my family's go-to veggies (broccoli) or a fresh green salad. A serving of your favorite pasta or slices of crusty bread can help to soak up all the heavenly sauce.

Slow Cooker Balsamic Chicken

Serves 4 to 6

10 boneless, skinless chicken thighs

1 sweet onion, coarsely chopped

4 cloves garlic, sliced

½ cup balsamic vinegar

3 tablespoons brown sugar

1 teaspoon Italian seasoning

½ teaspoon salt

¼ teaspoon black pepper

1 Place chicken thighs in the bottom of a 4-quart or larger slow cooker. Top with onion and garlic.

2 In a small bowl, combine balsamic vinegar, brown sugar, Italian seasoning, salt, and pepper. Pour over chicken and cook on LOW 6 hours or HIGH 3 hours or until chicken is fork-tender and internal temperature reaches 165 degrees.

Tina's Tip: *Your cooking time may vary based on the brand of slow cooker you have. So make sure you check that your chicken is cooked through and tender before digging in.*

Keep things simple and flavorful with a slow-cooked chicken dinner that's made with less than 10 ingredients. While I make this with boneless, skinless chicken breasts from time to time, I always come back to chicken thighs—they're so juicy! If you do prefer cooking with white meat, you'll only need about four to six chicken breasts, as they are larger than thighs.

Sheet Pan Chicken Supper

Serves 4 to 5

1 (0.7-ounce) packet Italian dressing mix

¼ cup vegetable oil

2-½ pounds bone-in, skin-on, split chicken breasts

12 ounces baby creamer potatoes, cut in half (see Tip)

1 cup cherry tomatoes

8 ounces fresh asparagus, trimmed and cut in half

1 Preheat oven to 400 degrees F.

2 In a large bowl, combine dressing mix and oil; mix well. Place chicken and potatoes on a rimmed baking sheet. Pour half of the oil mixture over chicken and potatoes, tossing to coat evenly. Roast 40 minutes, then remove from oven.

3 Add tomatoes and asparagus to remaining oil mixture; toss until evenly coated. Place vegetables all around chicken and potatoes. Roast 15 more minutes or until vegetables are fork-tender, and chicken is cooked through and internal temperature reaches 165 degrees. If the chicken is done before the vegetables, transfer chicken to a plate and cover with foil until ready to serve.

Tina's Tip: *Creamer potatoes are cute little baby potatoes. They're usually about an inch in diameter and come in golden or red varieties. When my potatoes are an inch in diameter or smaller, I usually leave them whole.*

I love cooking from scratch as often as possible. However, like most of you, there are many nights when I'm not opposed to using a supermarket shortcut. Rather than dealing with a bunch of spices, I grab an all-in-one seasoning packet, which is super convenient. Here, I use an Italian dressing mix to add lots of flavor to this one-pan meal. With all the seasoning I need in just one packet, all I have to do is add a protein, a few fresh veggies, and pop it into the oven.

Weeknight-Friendly Chicken Cacciatore

Serves 4 to 5

2 tablespoons olive oil

1-½ pounds boneless, skinless chicken breasts

½ teaspoon salt, plus extra to taste

¼ teaspoon black pepper

1 red bell pepper, cut into 1-inch chunks

1 onion, cut into 1-inch chunks

3 medium cloves garlic, minced

½ cup red wine

1 (24-ounce) jar marinara sauce

1 teaspoon Italian seasoning

Parmesan cheese for serving

1 In a large, deep skillet over medium-high heat, heat 2 tablespoons oil until hot. Sprinkle chicken lightly with salt and black pepper and brown in skillet 5 minutes per side. Remove chicken from skillet; set aside.

2 To the same skillet, add bell pepper, onion, and garlic; cook 2 minutes. Stir in wine and cook 1 minute or until wine reduces by half. Add remaining ingredients, return chicken to skillet, cover, and let simmer 35 to 40 minutes or until the chicken is very tender and you can pull it into bite-sized pieces. Add additional salt to taste. Serve with Parmesan cheese.

Tina's Tip: *Mushrooms are a popular addition to a cacciatore. If you're a fan, go ahead and add them to the recipe with the peppers and onion. The mushrooms should be thick-cut, so they don't disappear in your sauce.*

If you find yourself craving classic Italian dishes throughout the week, then you're going to love this easy take on an Italian favorite. It's simple to make at home and delivers restaurant-quality taste (especially if you opt for a high-quality marinara sauce). Serve over pasta or zucchini noodles for a quick and satisfying weeknight dinner.

Dill-icious Oven-Fried Chicken

Serves 5

½ cup all-purpose flour

4 cups cornflake cereal, crushed

⅓ cup grated Parmesan cheese

½ teaspoon salt

¼ teaspoon cayenne pepper

¼ teaspoon black pepper

¾ cup buttermilk

¼ cup pickle juice

1 (3-½- to 4-pound) chicken, cut into 10 pieces (see Tip)

Cooking spray

Tina's Tip: *To ensure that all your chicken pieces cook evenly, cut the chicken breasts in half. Not only do you end up with 2 more pieces, but that way all your pieces end up super-moist and crispy. Don't forget to add some sliced dill pickles for garnish!*

1 Preheat oven to 375 degrees. Line a rimmed baking sheet with aluminum foil and coat with cooking spray. Place a metal cooling rack on a baking sheet. (This will help make the chicken extra crispy.)

2 Place flour in a large resealable plastic bag. In another large resealable plastic bag, add crushed cornflakes, Parmesan cheese, salt, cayenne pepper, and black pepper; seal and shake well to combine.

3 Pour buttermilk into a shallow bowl. Add pickle juice and stir. Place 2 pieces of chicken in bag with flour; shake well to coat completely. Remove from bag, shaking to remove excess flour, and dip in buttermilk. Next, place into bag with cornflake mixture. Seal and shake well, coating chicken completely.

4 Place chicken on rack and repeat with remaining chicken. Sprinkle remaining cornflake mixture evenly over chicken on baking sheet. Lightly coat with cooking spray.

5 Bake 50 to 55 minutes or until chicken is no longer pink in center, internal temperature reaches 165 degrees, and crust is golden brown.

You may have noticed that my husband Lou and I are big pickle fans (check out my recipe for Southern "Fried" Pickles on page 36!), so it's no wonder that we're big fans of the pickle-topped chicken sandwiches they serve at Chick-Fil-A®. Rather than hitting the drive-through all the time, I found a way to recreate the dill-icious flavor at home. My version is baked, rather than fried, sowe can enjoy it more often.

Pennsylvania Dutch Chicken & Dumplings

Serves 5 to 6

2 celery stalks, thinly sliced

2 carrots, thinly sliced

8 cups chicken broth (regular or low sodium)

1 teaspoon poultry seasoning

¼ teaspoon black pepper

2 cups biscuit baking mix (see Tip)

⅔ cup milk

3 cups pulled cooked chicken

Salt to taste

1 Coat a soup pot with cooking spray and heat over medium-high heat. Add celery and carrots; sauté 6 minutes or until tender. Stir in broth, poultry seasoning, and pepper; bring to a boil.

2 Meanwhile, to make dumplings, in a medium bowl, stir together biscuit baking mix and milk until blended. Turn dough out onto a heavily floured surface; roll dough to ⅛-inch thickness. Cut into 1- x 3-inch strips.

3 Drop strips, a couple at a time, into boiling broth mixture, stirring gently. Add cooked chicken. Cover, reduce heat to low, and simmer 8 to 10 minutes, stirring occasionally, until dumplings are cooked through. Season with salt as desired.

Tina's Tip: *You can make your own substitute for biscuit baking mix with ingredients you probably have in your pantry. For the equivalent in this recipe, sift and whisk together 2 cups all-purpose flour, 3 teaspoons baking powder, and ½ teaspoon salt. Cut 2 tablespoons butter into the mixture until evenly combined, then use as directed above.*

There are basically two ways to make dumplings in a chicken and dumpling soup (and neither one is more "right" than the other). The first, which is how my mom used to make them, is more biscuit-like and involves dropping mounds of dough into the soup. The second version, known as "rolled" dumplings, are more noodle-like. They're the preferred version by the Pennsylvania Dutch. Since I went to college in the heart of Amish country, I got to know these dumplings very well. Now it's your turn to give this shortcut a try!

Bundt Pan Roasted Chicken

Serves 4 to 5

¼ cup olive oil

1 teaspoon onion powder

1 teaspoon garlic powder

1 teaspoon paprika

1 teaspoon kosher salt

¼ teaspoon black pepper

1 (3-½- to 4-pound) whole chicken

1 onion, cut into quarters

3 carrots, cut into 1-½-inch chunks

4 sprigs fresh thyme

½ cup chicken broth (regular or low sodium)

½ cup white wine

1 Preheat oven to 400 degrees F.

2 In a small bowl, mix together olive oil, onion powder, garlic powder, paprika, salt, and pepper. Rub inside and outside of chicken with mixture.

3 Slide tail end of chicken over hollow tube of a Bundt pan and place on a rimmed baking sheet. Arrange onion, carrots, and thyme in Bundt pan around chicken. Pour broth and wine into pan.

4 Roast 70 to 80 minutes, basting occasionally or until no longer pink and internal temperature reaches 165 degrees. Carefully remove chicken from Bundt pan, and allow to rest 5 minutes before cutting. Serve with veggies and pan drippings.

Tina's Tip: *Before you preheat your oven, make sure you lower your oven rack, so that there's enough room for the upright chicken. And don't toss your chicken carcass! You can save it in the freezer and use it to make homemade chicken stock.*

My husband loves roasted chicken. As a matter of fact, he would eat it every night if I made it for him. While I'm not ready to commit to a lifetime of daily roasted chicken, I'll admit that I love how easy it is to make, especially when it's prepared like this. The Bundt pan keeps the chicken super-moist and flavorful. Plus, I think the best part of this recipe is the juice that forms in the bottom of the pan. Make sure to have some crusty bread on hand for mopping it up.

Cornbread Taco Casserole

Serves 10 to 12

2 tablespoons vegetable oil

½ cup finely chopped onion

½ cup finely chopped red bell pepper

2 tablespoons all-purpose flour

1 cup chicken broth (regular or low sodium)

1 (16-ounce) jar salsa

1 (1-ounce) packet taco seasoning

3 cups shredded cooked chicken

1 (14.75 ounce) can creamed corn, divided

1 cup black beans, rinsed and drained

1 cup canned or frozen corn

1 (8.5-ounce) box cornbread mix

1 egg

½ stick butter, melted

4 cups crushed tortilla chips, divided

2 cups shredded cheddar cheese, divided

1 Preheat oven to 375 degrees F.

2 In a large deep skillet over medium heat, heat oil until hot. Sauté onion and red pepper about 5 minutes or until softened. Sprinkle with flour and stir. Stir in chicken broth, scraping up any bits from bottom of pan. Add salsa, taco seasoning, cooked chicken, half the creamed corn, the black beans, and corn. Bring mixture to a boil, reduce heat to low, and simmer 5 minutes, stirring occasionally.

3 In a bowl, stir together cornbread mix, remaining creamed corn, the egg, and melted butter.

4 Sprinkle 3 cups of crushed tortilla chips in bottom of a 9- x 13-inch baking dish. Top with the chicken mixture. Sprinkle with 1 cup of cheese. Spoon on dollops of cornbread mixture. Sprinkle with remaining 1 cup of cheese and remaining 1 cup of tortilla chips.

5 Bake, uncovered, 25 to 30 minutes or until cornbread mixture is golden brown and filling is bubbly.

Sometimes, to get a head start, I prepare the chicken filling ahead of time and refrigerate. Then I assemble the rest right before it's time to bake. (When you do this, the baking time will increase as the filling will be cold.) If you'd like, you can make this vegetarian by replacing the chicken with an additional 2 cups of black beans, swapping the chicken broth for vegetable broth, and doubling the corn. Serve with all of your favorite taco toppings.

Coconut Curry Chicken Skewers

Serves 4 to 6

16 (8-inch) wooden skewers
(see Tip)

Marinade

½ cup coconut milk

1 medium clove garlic, minced

1 teaspoon fresh ginger, minced

1 teaspoon curry powder

1-½ teaspoons brown sugar

1 tablespoon lime juice

½ teaspoon salt

1 pound boneless, skinless
chicken breasts, cut into
1-inch pieces

1 tablespoon vegetable oil

Peanut Dipping Sauce

1 cup coconut milk

½ cup creamy peanut butter

1 tablespoon curry powder

½ teaspoon fresh garlic, minced

½ teaspoon fresh ginger, minced

½ cup water

2 tablespoons lime juice

2 tablespoons soy sauce

1 In a resealable plastic bag, combine Marinade ingredients. Seal bag and shake until the sugar has dissolved and everything is mixed together. Add chicken to the bag, and marinate in the refrigerator at least 2 hours.

2 Coat a grill or grill pan with cooking spray and preheat to medium heat. Thread marinated chicken pieces onto skewers. Grill about 10 to 15 minutes or until no pink remains.

3 Meanwhile, to make the Peanut Dipping Sauce, in a saucepan over medium heat, mix together remaining 1 cup coconut milk, the peanut butter, curry powder, garlic, ginger and the water. Simmer 5 minutes or until smooth and thickened, stirring constantly. Remove from heat and stir in lime juice and soy sauce. Serve with chicken skewers.

Tina's Tip: *If grilling, it's a good idea to soak the skewers in water for about 20 minutes before threading on the chicken. It helps keep them from burning on grill. The finished skewers look pretty when garnished with some fresh minced cilantro, sliced green onions or chopped peanuts.*

These chicken skewers were a labor of love! I had to make and tweak lots of versions until I finally received my family's stamp of approval. If you're looking for a different way to prepare boneless skinless chicken breasts, this is certainly a fun and flavorful one. I hope they'll get your stamp of approval too!

Skillet Chicken & White Wine Mushrooms

Serves 4

¼ cup all-purpose flour

½ teaspoon salt,
plus more to taste

½ teaspoon black pepper

4 boneless, skinless chicken breasts (1 to 1-½ pounds total)

½ stick butter

½ pound mushrooms, quartered

1 small onion, chopped

¼ cup dry white wine

1 large tomato chopped

½ cup chicken broth (regular or low sodium)

1 tablespoon chopped fresh parsley

1 In a shallow dish, combine flour, salt, and pepper; coat chicken evenly on both sides.

2 In a large skillet over medium-high heat, melt butter; sauté chicken 4 to 5 minutes per side or until browned. Remove to a platter and set aside.

3 In the same skillet sauté mushrooms and onion, deglaze with wine, and cook 1 minute or until reduced by half. Add tomato and broth. Simmer 5 to 7 minutes, until vegetables are tender, stirring occasionally. Return chicken to skillet and reduce heat to medium-low.

4 Simmer 5 to 7 minutes or until sauce thickens, chicken is cooked through, and internal temperature of chicken reaches 165 degrees. Sprinkle with parsley and additional salt to taste.

Tina's Tip: *During the summer, when I find fresh leeks at the farmer's market, I often use them in place of the onion. I think they're an ingredient that is often underutilized, despite adding so much depth to almost any dish.*

Here is a dish to help you wine and dine your loved ones. I'm no stranger to cooking with mushrooms—in fact, I've entered the Kennett Square Mushroom Soup Cook-Off a few years (and even won first place a couple of times!). This is another way to showcase fresh mushrooms. It's an easy chicken dish that is packed with flavor and even looks a little fancy. You can use any kind of mushrooms you like, including white, cremini, or portobello.

Maui BBQ Chicken

Makes 4

4 boneless, skinless chicken breasts

½ teaspoon salt

¼ teaspoon black pepper

½ cup barbecue sauce

½ cup shredded mozzarella cheese

½ cup shredded smoked Gouda cheese

¼ cup thinly sliced red onion

¼ cup pineapple tidbits

2 tablespoons chopped fresh cilantro

1 Preheat oven to 400 degrees F. Coat a rimmed baking sheet with cooking spray.

2 Butterfly each chicken breast by placing it on a cutting board, and using a sharp knife, cutting in half horizontally about ¾ of the way through. (It should open like a book.) Cover the "opened" chicken breast with plastic wrap and gently flatten with a meat mallet until it's about ¼-inch thick. Repeat with remaining chicken.

3 Sprinkle both sides of chicken with salt and pepper and place on baking sheet. Bake 10 to 12 minutes or until no longer pink in center. Remove from oven and spread barbecue sauce evenly over each piece of chicken. Evenly sprinkle with cheeses, red onion, and pineapple.

4 Place back in oven and bake 4 to 5 more minutes or until cheese is melted. Sprinkle with cilantro and serve.

BBQ chicken pizza isn't for everybody, but I love it. This is basically a deconstructed version of the classic Hawaiian-style pie, but without the pizza crust. (If you want to pretend you're having pizza, cut your chicken into wedges—like I do in the photo!) You'll love this if you are following a low-carb diet or even if you aren't. Add a salad to your spread and dinner is done!

Simmering Greek Chicken

Serves 6

1 tablespoon olive oil

6 boneless, skinless, chicken breast cutlets (see Tip on page 99)

2 medium cloves garlic, minced

½ cup diced onion

3 tomatoes, diced

½ cup chicken broth (regular or low sodium)

½ cup Kalamata olives, coarsely chopped

½ teaspoon dried oregano

1 tablespoon chopped fresh parsley

½ teaspoon salt

¼ teaspoon black pepper

¼ cup feta cheese crumbles

1 In a large skillet over medium heat, heat oil until hot. Add chicken, in batches, and sauté 4 to 6 minutes or until golden, turning once during cooking. Remove chicken to a plate and set aside.

2 Add garlic and onion to skillet and sauté 3 to 4 minutes. Add tomatoes and broth; bring to a boil, then reduce heat to low and simmer 5 minutes.

3 Return chicken to skillet. Add olives, oregano, parsley, salt, and pepper and cook 2 to 3 minutes or until heated through and internal temperature of chicken reaches 165 degrees. Sprinkle with feta cheese and serve.

Tina's Tip: *Serve this with a side of lemony orzo and get ready for some good eating. To 3 cups hot cooked orzo, stir in 2 tablespoons butter, 2 tablespoons lemon juice, 1 teaspoon lemon zest, and 1 tablespoon chopped fresh parsley.*

When I was teaching 3rd grade, I had a student whose family made the best spanakopita ever. After telling them how much I loved it, they graciously shared their recipe with me. Let me tell you—it's a lot of work! Yet I still find myself making it almost every Easter. While I promised I would never share their family recipe, I am sharing this recipe for a Greek-inspired chicken dish that I often serve alongside it. It's tangy and delicious!

Italian-Stuffed Chicken Cutlets

Makes 6

6 boneless, skinless, chicken breast cutlets (see Tip)

½ teaspoon salt

¼ teaspoon black pepper

½ cup sundried tomatoes, chopped

3 ounces cream cheese, softened

¼ cup shredded mozzarella cheese

¼ cup prepared pesto

¾ cup Italian breadcrumbs

3 tablespoons grated Parmesan cheese

½ teaspoon paprika

Cooking spray

1 Preheat oven to 375 degrees F. Coat a baking sheet with cooking spray. Sprinkle chicken evenly with salt and pepper; set aside.

2 In a medium bowl, stir together sundried tomatoes, cream cheese, mozzarella cheese, and pesto. (If you want to make your own homemade pesto, see page 150.) Spread cheese mixture evenly over chicken breasts. Roll up like a jellyroll and secure with toothpicks.

3 In a shallow dish, combine breadcrumbs, Parmesan cheese, and paprika. Coat chicken in breadcrumb mixture. Place on baking sheet seam-side down and lightly spray chicken with cooking spray. (If time permits, I like to chill these for at least 30 minutes before baking as it prevents the filling from oozing out.)

4 Bake 20 to 25 minutes or until no longer pink in the center. Remove toothpicks and enjoy.

Tina's Tip: *Chicken cutlets and chicken breasts are one and the same. The difference is in the thickness. Chicken breasts are either cut in half horizontally or gently pounded out to make the thin cutlets. What's important to remember is that, for this recipe, you need the chicken thin enough that it can be rolled up. If you want to use regular chicken breasts, see page 96 for how to cut and pound the breasts into cutlets.*

Parmesan Turkey Patties

Makes 5

1 pound ground turkey breast

8 ounces Italian turkey sausage, with casing removed

⅓ cup panko breadcrumbs

⅓ cup grated Parmesan cheese

2 tablespoons finely minced onion

1 teaspoon Italian seasoning

¼ teaspoon garlic powder

¼ teaspoon salt

¼ teaspoon black pepper

2 tablespoons olive oil, divided

1-½ cups marinara sauce

1 cup shredded mozzarella cheese

1 In a large bowl, combine ground turkey, turkey sausage, breadcrumbs, Parmesan cheese, onion, Italian seasoning, garlic powder, salt, pepper, and 1 tablespoon oil. Form into 5 oval-shaped patties.

2 In a large skillet over medium heat, heat remaining 1 tablespoon oil. Brown patties about 3 minutes per side. Pour marinara sauce over patties, cover, and simmer about 5 minutes or until cooked through. Top each patty with mozzarella cheese; cover and heat 1 to 2 more minutes or until cheese is melted.

Tina's Tip: *If you love your cheese browned, like they make it in restaurants, you can finish these under the broiler. Right before serving, simply place them on a baking sheet for a minute or so until they're just the way you like them. No matter how you melt your cheese, finish these off with some fresh basil for an added burst of freshness.*

This is the perfect weeknight meal. It's super easy, and it comes together in under 30 minutes, which I love! We're big fans of turkey sausage, so adding some to the ground turkey breast along with grated Parmesan cheese adds tons of flavor and earns 2 thumbs up all around. We enjoy these with a side of zoodles (or pasta) and fluffy dinner rolls.

Herb-Brined Roasted Turkey

Serves 10 to 12

1 (17- to 20-pound) fresh or thawed turkey, brined (see next page)

1 lemon, quartered

1 onion, quartered

1 cup water

4 sprigs rosemary

6 sage leaves, plus extra for garnish

4 sprigs thyme

Canola oil

Tina's Tip: *My 17- to 20-pound turkey takes approximately 4 to 4-1/2 hours including resting time, so there's no reason to set your alarm clock for 3 am to get up and start cooking your turkey at that time, unless you plan to have turkey for breakfast. Lol!*

1 Preheat oven to 475 degrees F. Remove turkey from brine and discard brine. Rinse turkey inside and out with cold water. (You don't want any residual saltiness.) Place turkey on a roasting rack inside a large roasting pan and pat dry with paper towels.

2 Combine lemon, onion, and water in a microwave-safe dish. Cover and microwave on high 3 minutes. Place warmed onion and lemon, and the herbs inside turkey cavity. Tuck wings underneath turkey and tie legs together with kitchen twine. Coat skin with canola oil.

3 Roast turkey on lowest shelf of oven for 30 minutes.

4 Insert an oven-safe thermometer into thickest part of turkey breast and reduce temperature to 350 degrees. Roast 10 to 15 minutes per pound, basting every 30 minutes. If turkey becomes too dark, loosely cover with foil.

5 Roast until thickest part of breast is 160 to 165 degrees. When turkey is done, remove from oven, loosely cover with foil, and let rest 20 to 30 minutes before carving.

This is my go-to Thanksgiving turkey recipe. After brining the turkey for almost a full day, the turkey is ready for roasting with plenty of fresh herbs, lemon, and onion. If you've never been successful with making moist turkey at home, I strongly recommend you give my recipe a try at your next holiday dinner.

Flavorful Turkey Brine

Makes enough for up to a 20-pound turkey

16 cups low-sodium chicken broth

1 cup coarse kosher salt

½ cup light brown sugar

1 tablespoon black peppercorns

3 bay leaves

1 lemon, zested and quartered

3 cloves garlic, roughly chopped

3 sprigs rosemary

3 sprigs thyme

1 sprig sage, about 8 leaves

1 gallon heavily iced water

Several bags of ice, if using cooler method

Tina's Tip: *If you don't have room in your fridge, you could also place the sealed bag into a large sanitized cooler. Cover it generously with ice and tightly close the cover. It's important that the turkey stays cold during the brining. I would also recommend sanitizing the cooler after you're done, too.*

1 To make the brine, in a large stockpot over medium-high heat, combine chicken broth, salt, brown sugar, peppercorns, bay leaves, lemon zest, lemon quarters, garlic, rosemary, thyme, and sage. Stir occasionally to dissolve solids and bring to a boil. Remove brine from heat, cool to room temperature, and refrigerate. (Make sure you do this at least a day before, as you want to brine your turkey for at least 8 to 16 hours, and you still need time to cook it.)

2 Make sure to remove any innards from inside the turkey.

3 Using a container, brining bag or oven bag, (if using a bag, place bag into a roasting pan first) put turkey into container or bag. Pour the cooled brine over the turkey and immediately add a gallon of ice water to the container or bag and seal it.

4 Refrigerate or keep in cooler 8 to 16 hours.

Brining is the perfect way to ensure that your turkey will be packed with flavor, super juicy and the talk of your Thanksgiving meal. The brine makes the turkey so moist and flavorful! This makes enough brine for one turkey.

Beef & Pork

Ramen Noodle Steak Bowl 106

My Go-To Meatloaf 108

Unstuffed Stuffed Pepper Casserole 110

Chianti & Rosemary Beef Stew 111

Horseradish-Kissed Pot Roast 112

Cheddar-Crusted Cottage Pie 114

Meatball & Ricotta Hoagies 116

Sweet & Sour Short Ribs with Cabbage 117

Open-Faced Steakhouse Special 118

Salami & Fontina Hamburgers 120

Roasted Pork with Pineapple-Pepper Jelly 122

Honey-Garlic Pork Tenderloin 123

Slow Cooker Sausage & Bean One-Pot 124

Foil Packet Pierogi Dinner 125

Potato-Crusted Pork Chops 126

Easy Egg Roll in a Bowl 128

Barbecued Baby Back Ribs 129

Ramen Noodle Steak Bowl

Serves 4

1 (12-ounce) strip steak

½ teaspoon salt

¼ teaspoon black pepper

2 teaspoons sesame oil

1 tablespoon grated fresh ginger

2 medium cloves garlic, minced

2 cups sliced mushrooms (shitake if available)

1 carrot, thinly sliced

4 cups beef broth (regular or low sodium)

1 tablespoon soy sauce, plus more to taste

2 cups broccoli florets

2 baby bok choy, cut in half

2 (3-ounce) packages ramen noodles (discard seasoning packets)

4 medium soft-boiled eggs, cut in half (see Tip)

Sliced scallions and sesame seeds for garnish (optional)

1 Season steak with salt and pepper. Coat a grill pan or skillet with cooking spray and over medium heat, cook steak 5 to 6 minutes on each side for medium or until desired doneness. Remove steak to a plate and let rest.

2 Meanwhile, in a soup pot over medium heat, add oil, ginger, garlic, mushrooms, and carrots. Sauté 3 to 4 minutes or until carrots are tender. Add broth and soy sauce and bring to a boil. Toss in broccoli, and bok choy; cover and cook 2 to 3 minutes or until vegetables are tender. Add ramen noodles and cook 3 minutes more or until noodles are tender. Add more soy sauce to taste.

3 Divide soup into bowls and arrange veggies. Slice steak thinly across the grain and arrange on top of each bowl. Top with eggs. Garnish with scallions and sesame seeds, if desired.

Tina's Tip: *For the perfect, medium, soft-boiled eggs, place eggs in a pot and cover with cold water. Place the pot over high heat until it comes to a boil. Once boiling, set a timer for 6 minutes. After 6 minutes, remove the eggs from the pot and place them into a bowl of ice water to prevent overcooking. Carefully peel eggs, cut in half, and serve.*

My husband and I love going out for ramen, but we like making it at home even more since it allows us to customize our bowls. We've even gotten the girls on board, so now we slurp down our noodles as a family.

My Go-To Meatloaf

Serves 4 to 6

2 tablespoons vegetable oil

1 cup finely chopped mushrooms

1 cup finely chopped onion

3 small cloves garlic, minced

3 slices white bread, torn into small pieces

¼ cup milk

1-½ pounds ground beef

1 egg

1 tablespoon steak sauce

1 teaspoon salt

¼ teaspoon black pepper

1 In a skillet over medium heat, heat oil until hot. Add mushrooms, onion, and garlic. Sauté 6 to 8 minutes or until mixture starts to soften; set aside.

2 Preheat oven to 350 degrees F.

3 Meanwhile, in a large bowl, using your hands or a hand or stand mixer on low, combine bread and milk and let sit 5 minutes so that the bread absorbs the milk. Add remaining ingredients, including the mushroom, onion, and garlic mixture. Mix until evenly combined, but don't overmix or your meatloaf will be tough. Place mixture on a rimmed baking sheet and form into an oval loaf shape.

4 Bake 60 to 65 minutes or until no pink remains, juices run clear, and internal temperature reaches 160 degrees. Allow meatloaf to rest 5 minutes, then slice into 1-inch slices and serve.

Tina's Tip: *If you want to take this meatloaf over the top, try serving it with my Marsala Mushroom Gravy. To make it, all you have to do is sauté 1/4 cup finely chopped onion and 3/4 cup sliced mushrooms in 2 tablespoons of oil. Cook 5 to 7 minutes or until veggies are tender. Add 1/4 teaspoon dried thyme and 3 tablespoons flour; stir to combine. Add 1/4 cup Marsala wine, scraping up any bits from the pan. Stir in 1-1/2 cups beef broth, 1/4 teaspoon salt, and 1/8 teaspoon black pepper. Cook 3 to 5 minutes or until thickened. Spoon over meatloaf and enjoy.*

Unstuffed Stuffed Pepper Casserole

Serves 4 to 5

1 tablespoon vegetable oil

1 bell pepper (any color),
cut into ½-inch chunks

½ cup chopped onion

1 pound ground beef

1 (15-ounce) can tomato sauce

2 cups cooked rice (see Tip)

1 cup shredded mozzarella
cheese, divided

1 teaspoon finely chopped garlic

1 teaspoon Italian seasoning

¾ teaspoon salt

½ teaspoon black pepper

1 Preheat oven to 350 degrees F. Coat a 2-quart baking dish with cooking spray.

2 In a large skillet over medium-high heat, heat oil until hot. Sauté bell pepper and onion 4 to 5 minutes or until veggies are tender. Add ground beef and cook an additional 6 to 8 minutes or until no pink remains in beef. Drain excess fat from skillet.

3 Add tomato sauce, rice, ½ cup mozzarella cheese, the garlic, Italian seasoning, salt, and pepper; mix well. Spoon into baking dish and cover with aluminum foil.

4 Bake 25 to 30 minutes or until heated through. Remove foil and sprinkle with remaining cheese. Bake 5 more minutes or until cheese is melted.

Tina's Tip: *If you're pressed for time, you can use frozen cooked rice. Just thaw and add as directed in the recipe.*

Truth be told, not everyone (I won't mention any names!) in our house is a huge fan of traditional stuffed peppers, so I don't spend a lot of time making them the traditional way. Instead, I prefer this version, which is much easier and perfect for weeknight dinners. Plus, my family loves the cheesy goodness in every bite.

Chianti & Rosemary Beef Stew

Serves 6 to 8

5 tablespoons all-purpose flour, divided

2 pounds beef cubes for stew

2 tablespoons vegetable oil

¾ cup Chianti or other dry red wine

3-½ cups beef broth (regular or low sodium)

1 teaspoon salt

½ teaspoon black pepper

1 large onion, cut into 1-inch chunks

4 carrots, cut into 1-inch chunks

5 potatoes, peeled and cut into 1-½-inch chunks

3 cloves garlic, chopped

2 tablespoons tomato paste

2 sprigs rosemary

2 tablespoons butter, softened

1 Preheat oven to 350 degrees F.

2 In a large resealable plastic bag, combine 3 tablespoons flour and the beef; toss until beef is evenly coated. In a Dutch oven or other oven-safe pot, over medium-high heat, heat oil until hot. Brown beef on all sides (in batches, if necessary), stirring occasionally. Add wine and broth, scraping bits from bottom of pot to deglaze. Bring to simmer, cover pot, and place in oven to braise for 30 minutes.

3 Remove from oven and add salt, pepper, onion, carrots, potatoes, garlic, wine, tomato paste, and rosemary. Cover pot and place back in oven for 1-¼ to 1-½ hours, or until beef is tender. Remove rosemary stems and discard.

4 In a small bowl, mix remaining 2 tablespoons flour with butter; add a small amount of the stew broth and mix until smooth and pourable. Slowly pour into stew and stir until combined. Let simmer over low heat on the stovetop 5 to 8 minutes or until thickened.

Tina's Tip: *If you have any leftover tomato paste, rather than placing the open can in the fridge and forgetting about it, here's what to do: Get out some wax paper and lay it over a baking sheet. Then place tablespoon portions of tomato paste over the wax paper and freeze. Once the portions have firmed up, peel from the wax paper and place them in a resealable freezer bag. Then when you need some tomato paste, just grab what you need. (The paste can be kept frozen for up to one year.)*

My daughter, Sam, has always loved beef stew. We used to joke about getting her a t-shirt that read: "I ♥ Beef Stew." As a result of her love for beef stew, I've made a lot of them over the years. This one is flavorful, tender, and family-approved. (Sorry Sam, hope this doesn't embarrass you!)

Horseradish-Kissed Pot Roast

Serves 6 to 8

1 (3 pound) chuck roast

1 teaspoon salt

1 teaspoon black pepper

2 tablespoons vegetable oil

3 sweet onions, peeled and quartered

1 cup beef broth (regular or low sodium)

1 (8-ounce) jar prepared horseradish (not the creamed style)

3 carrots, cut into 2-inch pieces

2 tablespoons butter, softened

2 tablespoons all-purpose flour

Tina's Tip: *The cooking time for this can vary greatly depending on how thick your chuck roast is. A thicker piece might take an additional ½ hour as opposed to a flatter cut, even through they may both weigh the same amount.*

1 Preheat oven to 300 degrees F.

2 Season roast with salt and pepper. In a 5 to 6 quart oven-safe Dutch oven over medium-high heat, heat oil until hot. Brown roast on both sides and remove to a plate. Add onions to pot and cook 2 to 3 minutes, stirring occasionally. Add broth, scraping up browned bits from bottom of the pot, to deglaze.

3 Place roast back in pot on top of onions. Spread horseradish over top of roast. Bring to a simmer, then cover and place in oven.

4 Cook in oven 1-¼ hours. Remove from oven and add carrots around roast. Return to oven and cook 45 minutes more or until meat is fork-tender. Remove roast to a platter and pull into chunks using 2 forks. Place carrots around meat to serve.

5 To make a gravy, place Dutch oven back on stove; skim off excess fat from broth in the Dutch oven. In a small bowl, mix the butter and flour with a fork to form a paste. Spoon a few tablespoons of the broth into the paste and stir until smooth. Stir the butter-flour mixture into the broth and let it simmer over low heat, 2 to 3 minutes or until thickened, stirring occasionally.

This is a roast I make all the time. Most people see "horseradish" and automatically think "spicy," but in this recipe the horseradish mellows during the long cooking time and simply adds tons of flavor to the roast. You can serve this alongside some creamy mashed potatoes or buttery polenta. Add some green peas for a burst of color.

Cheddar-Crusted Cottage Pie

Serves 5 to 6

1-½ pounds ground beef

½ cup chopped onion

1 teaspoon chopped garlic

½ teaspoon salt

½ teaspoon black pepper

¼ cup all-purpose flour

2 cups beef broth (regular or low sodium)

1 cup frozen peas and carrots

1 cup frozen corn

1 tablespoon fresh chopped thyme, plus extra for sprinkling

4 cups prepared mashed potatoes (see Tip)

1 cup shredded cheddar cheese

1 Preheat oven to 375 degrees F.

2 In 10- to 12-inch cast iron or ovenproof skillet over medium-high heat, sauté beef, onion, and garlic 5 minutes or until browned. Drain excess fat, if needed. Stir in salt, pepper, and flour; cook 1 minute. Slowly stir in beef broth, peas and carrots, corn, and 1 tablespoon thyme; bring to a boil, stirring occasionally. When mixture starts to thicken, remove from heat.

3 In a medium bowl, combine mashed potatoes and cheese; mix well. Spoon potato mixture over top of meat mixture and spread not quite to the edges.

4 Bake 30 to 35 minutes or until heated through and potato-cheese mixture starts to turn golden. Sprinkle with more chopped thyme and serve.

Tina's Tip: *When it comes to the mashed potatoes, you can make your favorite kind or use a package of refrigerated, prepared mashed potatoes. (They're easy and weeknight-friendly.) This is also delicious with my Cheesy Cauliflower and Potato Mash on page 174.*

It's hard to go wrong with something as comforting as ground beef and mashed potatoes. Aside from being such a warm and welcoming meal, I love that there's minimal prep work and only one pan to wash. It's also a great way to use up leftover mashed potatoes, so save this one for after those big holiday dinners.

Meatball & Ricotta Hoagies

Makes 4

1 pound ground beef

¾ cup breadcrumbs

½ cup grated Parmesan cheese

½ cup milk

¼ cup chopped fresh parsley

1 egg

1 teaspoon fresh minced garlic
or 1 teaspoon garlic powder

1 teaspoon salt

1 teaspoon black pepper

2 (26-ounce) jars marinara sauce

4 hoagie rolls, split (see Tip)

1 cup ricotta cheese

Fresh slivered basil for sprinkling

1 In a large mixing bowl, using your hands or an electric mixer on low, combine beef, breadcrumbs, Parmesan cheese, milk, parsley, egg, garlic powder, salt, and pepper; gently mix until evenly combined. (Mixing gently is the key to tender meatballs.) Form mixture into 12 meatballs and place in a large, heavy-bottomed soup pot. Add marinara sauce and stir gently to ensure all meatballs are coated with sauce.

2 Bring to a boil over medium heat, then reduce heat to low. Cover loosely and simmer 25 to 30 minutes, or until meatballs are cooked through, stirring occasionally.

3 Place 3 meatballs on each roll, spoon on some sauce, dollop with ricotta cheese, and add a sprinkle of basil.

Tina's Tip: *I like to toast the rolls beforehand, so each hoagie has a nice crunch to it. Sometimes I'll slather the inside of the rolls with garlic butter before toasting them to add an extra burst of garlicky goodness.*

I've been making meatballs for as long as I can remember. Last year, I even started experimenting with grinding my own beef too. (KitchenAid® has a great attachment for this!) One way to enjoy meatballs is inside a hoagie (a Philly favorite!). These are perfect for game day or anytime you have people over. The addition of ricotta cheese makes them a little different, but so delicious!

Sweet & Sour Short Ribs with Cabbage

Serves 4 to 6

1 tablespoon vegetable oil

4 pounds beef chuck short ribs

¾ teaspoon salt

½ teaspoon black pepper

1 (28-ounce) can crushed tomatoes

1 (6-ounce) can tomato paste

2 tablespoons lemon juice

6 cups beef broth (regular or low sodium)

⅔ cup packed brown sugar

½ of a large cabbage, coarsely chopped (about 5 cups)

Lemon wedges for serving (optional)

1 In a soup pot over medium-high heat, heat oil until hot. Sprinkle short ribs with salt and pepper and sear 6 to 8 minutes or until browned on all sides. Drain off pan drippings.

2 Add remaining ingredients, except cabbage, and bring to a boil. Reduce heat to low and simmer, uncovered, 1-½ hours.

3 Add cabbage and simmer an additional hour or until ribs are fork-tender, stirring occasionally. Serve with lemon wedges, if desired.

The best way to cook short ribs is low and slow—that's how you end up with fork-tender meat. These are cooked in an amazing sweet and sour sauce that pairs perfectly with slices of hearty bread—so you can soak it all up! When it's done, I like to add an extra squeeze of fresh lemon juice. It adds a finishing touch that brightens up the flavors in the meal.

Open-Faced Steakhouse Special

Serves 4

2 tablespoons light brown sugar

2 teaspoons smoked paprika

2 teaspoons kosher salt, plus extra for sprinkling

¼ teaspoon black pepper, plus extra for sprinkling

¼ teaspoon cayenne pepper

2 rib eye steaks (about 1-½ pounds total)

1 tablespoon finely minced garlic

1 sweet onion, cut into ¼-inch-thick slices

8 (½-inch-thick) slices sourdough bread

½ cup olive oil

Tina's Tip: *To make a quick, tasty sauce to serve along with this recipe, combine 1 cup plain Greek yogurt, 2 cloves garlic, minced, 2 teaspoons lemon juice, 1 teaspoon kosher salt 1/4 teaspoon black pepper, and 1 tablespoon chopped fresh parsley; mix well. Refrigerate until ready to serve.*

1 In a small bowl, combine brown sugar, paprika, 2 teaspoons salt, ¼ teaspoon black pepper, and the cayenne pepper; mix well. Rub steaks evenly on both sides with garlic. Sprinkle spice mixture evenly over both sides of steaks, then pat gently to make sure spices stick. Set aside to rest.

2 Coat grill with cooking spray and preheat to medium heat (see note). Place steaks on grill and cook 9 to 14 minutes, flipping halfway through for medium doneness (145 degrees) or until desired doneness. Remove steaks to a platter, cover with foil, and allow to rest.

3 Meanwhile, brush onion slices and bread evenly with olive oil and lightly sprinkle with salt and black pepper. Place onion slices on grill, cover, and cook 1 to 2 minutes or until they start to brown. Turn over and cook 1 to 2 more minutes or until onions are tender and golden. During the last few minutes of cooking the onions, toast both sides of bread on grill. (Keep an eye on them, since they'll toast pretty quickly.)

4 Thinly slice steak across the grain and serve on the toasted bread. Top with onions and drizzle with any collected steak juices.

Note: If you prefer, this can be cooked inside on an electric grill or on a grill pan.

This is twist on a recipe that I entered in a steak cook-off where I was a finalist. It was such a hit that I wanted you to be able to experience it too.

Salami & Fontina Hamburgers

Makes 4

1-½ pounds ground beef

1 tablespoon Worcestershire sauce

½ teaspoon salt

½ teaspoon black pepper

4 slices fontina cheese

8 slices Genoa salami

4 ciabatta rolls, split in half

Olive oil for brushing

1 cup arugula

1 Preheat grill to medium-high. In a large bowl, combine ground beef, Worcestershire sauce, salt, and pepper; gently mix until combined. Shape mixture into 4 patties. Make an indentation in the center of each burger with your thumb. (This helps the burger keep its shape while cooking, without puffing up.)

2 Cook burgers 4 to 5 minutes per side for medium, or until desired doneness. Top each burger with a slice of cheese and heat until melted. At the same time, place salami on grill and heat 1 to 2 minutes or until lightly grilled, turning once during cooking.

3 Meanwhile, brush cut sides of rolls lightly with oil; place on grill, cut-side down, and toast about 1 minute or until golden. Top toasted rolls with arugula, salami, burgers, and my yummy aioli. (See Tip.)

Tina's Tip: *I like to serve this with a homemade Roasted Pepper Aioli. To make: in a food processor or blender, combine 1 cup of well-drained roasted peppers, ¾ cup mayonnaise, 3 small cloves garlic, ½ teaspoon salt, and ¼ teaspoon black pepper, and pulse until almost smooth.*

My father-in-law, Jim, loves this burger. He's Italian and will add salami to just about anything, so a burger like this is right up his alley. It's also a good change from your standard, American-cheese-and-sesame-bun-style burger. While it might get you the side eye from some of the traditionalists in your life, once they take a bite they'll be sold. It is just too delicious to resist.

Roasted Pork with Pineapple-Pepper Jelly

Serves 6 to 8

1 (4- to 5-pound) boneless
pork shoulder

1 tablespoon salt

1 teaspoon black pepper

2 teaspoons garlic powder

Pineapple-Pepper Jelly

1 cup pineapple preserves

½ cup jalapeño pepper jelly

½ cup light brown sugar

1 Preheat oven to 300 degrees F. Place pork on a large piece of foil and evenly season on all sides with salt, pepper, and garlic powder. Seal foil tightly and place in a roasting pan. Cook 3-½ hours or until internal temperature is 145 degrees.

2 Let pork rest 5 minutes before carefully unwrapping. (It's going to be steaming hot.) Using 2 forks, pull apart into chunks. (If meat does not pull apart, re-wrap with foil and roast another 30 minutes.) Once tender, pull apart into chunks, place on a platter, and pour pan juices over the top.

3 Meanwhile, to make Pineapple-Pepper Jelly, in a small saucepan over low heat, combine pineapple preserves, pepper jelly, and brown sugar. Stir just until sugar is dissolved and mixture is hot. Serve sauce with pork and enjoy.

Tina's Tip: *If you're having a hard time finding pineapple preserves, you can try other preserve varieties—like mango or apricot.*

The beauty of this recipe is that it allows you to serve up a taste of the tropics any time of the year, which means that even if it's snowing out, you can make this for dinner and dream of island breezes. I like to serve this with yellow rice and black beans to round out my tropical dining experience.

Honey-Garlic Pork Tenderloin

Serves 5 to 6

½ cup honey

¼ cup soy sauce

¼ cup lemon juice

5 cloves garlic, chopped

2 pork tenderloins, trimmed
(about 1-½ pounds total)

1 In a shallow dish or resealable plastic bag, mix together all ingredients except pork; remove 1 cup of mixture to a bowl and reserve for basting.

2 Pierce pork several times with a fork (this will ensure that all the marinade penetrates the meat) and add to dish or bag. Cover and chill 1 hour, turning halfway through marinating time.

3 Preheat grill to medium. (See Tip.) Remove pork from marinade, discarding excess marinade.

4 Place pork on grill, cover grill, and cook pork 11 to 13 minutes per side, or until internal temperature is 145 degrees and pork is slightly pink, basting occasionally with reserved marinade. Let rest 10 minutes, then slice into ¼-inch slices and enjoy.

Tina's Tip: *No grill? No problem! I've made this inside in a grill pan or skillet with amazing results. This is also a great option when the weather isn't cooperating.*

This is an easy and delicious way to prepare pork tenderloin. I like using this cut of pork because it's budget-friendly, cooks fairly quickly, and can be really tender and flavorful when not overcooked. Go ahead and serve this versatile dish with any of your favorite sides, or try pairing it with my Bacon-Wrapped Green Bean Bundles on page 164.

Slow Cooker Sausage & Bean One-Pot

Serves 4 to 6

2 carrots, chopped

1 cup chopped onion

4 cloves garlic, minced

6 sprigs thyme, leaves removed

½ teaspoon black pepper

8 ounces dried Great Northern beans

1 pound Italian sausage links

1 (14.5-ounce) can diced tomatoes

4 cups low-sodium chicken broth

½ cup ditalini pasta

4 cups fresh spinach

2 teaspoons balsamic vinegar

Parmesan cheese for sprinkling

Salt to taste

1 In a 5-quart or larger slow cooker, place carrots, onion, garlic, thyme, pepper, beans, and sausage. Pour tomatoes and chicken broth over sausage. Cover and cook on HIGH 4 hours or on LOW 7 hours or until beans are tender.

2 Remove sausage to a cutting board and cut into 1-inch chunks. Place back into slow cooker. Stir in pasta, spinach, and balsamic vinegar. Cover and continue to cook on HIGH 20 to 25 minutes or until pasta is tender. Sprinkle with Parmesan cheese and salt to taste.

Tina's Tip: *Keep in mind that any time you use a slow cooker, the cooking time may vary depending on which brand you use. Also, I do recommend using low-sodium broth as it concentrates while cooking in this dish.*

If you're craving a meal that delivers that homey, comfort food feel, this super easy one-pot is for you. It is great for those days when you know you're not going to have a lot of time to get dinner on the table, yet you still want something that's homemade, yummy, and belly-warming. It's all thanks to a trusty slow cooker.

Foil Packet Pierogi Dinner

Makes 4

¾ cup Italian vinaigrette dressing (see Tip)

1 tablespoon Dijon mustard

8 ounces kielbasa sausage, cut into ½-inch slices

12 frozen mini potato and cheese pierogi, thawed

½ red bell pepper, cut into ½-inch chunks

4 ounces fresh French green beans, ends trimmed

½ cup coarsely chopped onion

1 Preheat oven to 400 degrees F. Cut 4 (12-inch) squares of aluminum foil.

2 In a large bowl, whisk Italian dressing and mustard. Add remaining ingredients and stir until evenly coated. Divide mixture evenly onto center of each piece of foil. Wrap foil securely, leaving room for steam to circulate while cooking; seal edges tightly.

3 Place packets on a rimmed baking sheet. Bake 20 minutes or until vegetables are tender. Open packets carefully, as steam will be very, very hot. Serve immediately.

Tina's Tip: *If I have the time, I start with a homemade Italian dressing (see page 158). Also, another cooking option would be to place these packets on a grill over medium heat for 8 to 10 minutes or until heated through.*

I really love pierogi. They bring back memories of the delicious pierogi the ladies would make at our church bazaars. If you've never had them before, they are basically little dumplings filled with all different kinds of savory fillings. Fortunately, you can find frozen varieties at almost any grocery store (and if they don't have the mini kind, the regular-sized ones are fine too). I hope this recipe brings some pierogi joy into your life!

Potato-Crusted Pork Chops

Serves 4

2 eggs

2 tablespoons water

1-½ cups dried instant potato flakes (see Tip)

½ teaspoon paprika

4 (4-ounce) boneless pork chops, lightly pounded to ¼-inch-thickness

½ teaspoon salt

¼ teaspoon black pepper

¼ cup olive oil, divided

Shredded cheddar cheese for topping

Sour cream for topping

Crumbled cooked bacon for topping

Chives for topping

1 In a shallow dish, beat eggs with water. Place potato flakes and paprika in another shallow dish; mix well. Season pork chops evenly with salt and pepper. Dip pork chops in egg mixture, letting excess drip back into the dish. Dredge pork chops in potato flakes, pressing lightly to make sure coating sticks well.

2 In a large skillet over medium heat, heat 2 tablespoons olive oil until hot. Working in batches, add pork chops to skillet and cook 2 to 3 minutes per side or until crispy and golden, adding more oil as needed. Remove pork chops to a paper towel-lined platter and cover with foil to keep warm until all are cooked.

3 Serve pork and set out toppings, so that everyone can customize their own.

Tina's Tip: *Dried potato flakes, also known as instant mashed potatoes, are made from dehydrated cooked potatoes. They are a tasty alternative to bread crumbs (and they're gluten-free).*

I can eat a juicy pork chop or a loaded baked potato just about any day, so combining the two was a no-brainer. This is a main dish that everyone in my family loves, especially because they get to make it their own. Get your veggies in by serving alongside some green beans and enjoy!

Easy Egg Roll in a Bowl

Serves 4

2 tablespoons soy sauce, plus more to taste

1 teaspoon fresh grated ginger (see Tip)

1 teaspoon fresh minced garlic (see Tip)

¼ teaspoon black pepper

2 teaspoons peanut oil (see Tip)

½ pound ground pork

1 (16-ounce) package coleslaw mix

2 scallions, sliced

¼ cup sweet Thai chili sauce

1 In a small bowl, combine 2 tablespoons soy sauce, ginger, garlic, and pepper; mix well and set aside.

2 In a large skillet over medium-high heat, heat oil until hot; cook pork 5 to 7 minutes or until no longer pink, stirring occasionally. Add coleslaw, scallions, chili sauce, and soy sauce mixture to skillet. Mix well and cook 2 to 3 minutes or just until cabbage begins to soften. Add more soy sauce to taste.

Tina's Tip: *You can swap out the fresh ginger for 1/2 teaspoon ground ginger, and the fresh garlic for 1/2 teaspoon garlic powder. Oh, and we enjoy this with brown rice and topped with some Sriracha sauce!*

This is probably one of the easiest, throw-together dinners in my book—and it's really, really good. There are so many great flavors that bring this Asian-inspired dish together, like ginger, soy, and sweet Thai chili sauce. On occasion, I'll even add some crunch to each bowl by topping with crispy wonton strips, which you can usually find next to the other salad toppers in your grocery store. Roasted peanuts are great too!

Barbecued Baby Back Ribs

Serves 3 to 4

4 to 5 pounds pork baby back ribs

1 teaspoon garlic powder

1 teaspoon smoked paprika

1 teaspoon salt

½ teaspoon black pepper

Homemade Barbecue Sauce

1 cup ketchup

1 small onion, finely chopped

¼ cup firmly packed light brown sugar

2 tablespoons white vinegar

2 tablespoons Worcestershire sauce

2 tablespoons prepared yellow mustard

1 Preheat oven to 300 degrees F. Place ribs meat-side up in a large roasting pan.

2 In a small bowl, combine garlic powder, paprika, salt, and pepper. Season ribs with spice mixture, then cover tightly with aluminum foil; cook 2-½ hours.

3 Meanwhile, in a medium bowl, combine ingredients for Homemade Barbecue Sauce and mix well; set aside.

4 Right before serving, preheat grill to medium-high heat. Brush ribs with sauce and cook on grill until sauce begins to caramelize. Cut into individual ribs and serve with remaining sauce.

Tina's Tip: *If grilling isn't an option for you, you can place the ribs on a couple of rimmed baking sheets that have been covered with foil (so that clean-up is a breeze). Then slather the ribs with the sauce. Cook them for about 20 minutes in a 450-degree oven, or until the sauce starts to caramelize, basting occasionally.*

Nothing beats a plate of barbecued ribs at a cookout, especially barbecued ribs that are slathered in homemade barbecue sauce. Set out a big stack of napkins, because these are messy (in a deliciously good way!). If you are serving these at a cookout, you'll also want to include some of your favorite cookout sides. (One of my favorites is my Best-of-Both-Worlds Potato Salad on page 179.)

Seafood, Pasta, & More

Poached Shrimp with Tropical Fruit Salsa 132

Crispy-Coated Crab Cakes 134

Brown Sugar Glazed Salmon 136

Greek-Style Grouper 138

Fri-Yay Fish Tacos 139

Creamy Lemon Shrimp 140

Three-in-One Homemade Pasta 142

All-American Mac & Cheese 144

Chicken Rigatoni with Creamy Marinara 146

Veggie Lover's Lasagna 147

Cheesy Sausage Stuffed Shells 148

Pesto & Peppers Cheese Tortellini 150

Supreme Stuffed Portobello Mushrooms 152

Easy Classic Pizza Dough 153

Mama Mia's Meatball Pizza 154

Fig, Prosciutto, and Arugula Flatbread 156

Balsamic Veggie Stacks 158

Poached Shrimp with Tropical Fruit Salsa

Serves 3 to 4

10 cups cold water

2 celery stalks, quartered

1 large onion, quartered

3 cloves garlic, cut in half

1 lemon, cut in half

5 sprigs fresh thyme

1 tablespoon salt

1 pound raw, extra-large shrimp in shell

Tropical Fruit Salsa

½ red bell pepper

¼ red onion

¼ cup fresh parsley

½ cup pineapple chunks

2 mangoes, peeled and pit removed

1 tablespoon lime juice

½ teaspoon salt

⅛ teaspoon cayenne pepper

1 In a large pot over high heat, combine water, celery, onion, garlic, lemon, thyme, and salt; bring to a boil. Reduce heat to low and simmer 20 minutes, loosely covering the pot. (This is going to make a great flavorful broth to poach the shrimp in.)

2 Place shrimp in broth and turn off heat. Allow to poach 2 to 3 minutes or until shrimp turn pink, stirring once. Drain well and let cool. Peel shrimp, leaving tails on. Refrigerate until chilled.

3 Meanwhile, in a food processor, combine ingredients for Tropical Fruit Salsa and pulse until finely chopped. Refrigerate until chilled. Serve with shrimp and enjoy.

Tina's Tip: *If you want to add a bit more spice to your salsa, you can always add half of a seeded jalapeño to the food processor, along with all the other yummy stuff. Since I love fresh cilantro, I often substitute it for the fresh parsley.*

Summer entertaining calls for light and refreshing entrees, like this one. Not only is the shrimp flavorful on its own, but when paired with the fruity salsa, it tastes extraordinary. (I love mango—fresh, frozen, or dried—it's one of my favorites.) Just because my husband is allergic to shellfish, doesn't mean he can't enjoy this one. We just set some salsa aside for him and he digs in with chips!

Crispy-Coated Crab Cakes

Makes 5

½ cup mayonnaise

2 eggs, divided

1 tablespoon Dijon mustard

½ teaspoon seafood seasoning (like Old Bay®)

½ teaspoon salt

¼ teaspoon black pepper

1-½ cups panko breadcrumbs, divided

¼ cup finely chopped celery

1 pound lump crabmeat

4 tablespoons canola oil

1 In a large bowl, whisk together mayonnaise, 1 egg, mustard, seafood seasoning, salt, and pepper. Add ¾ cup breadcrumbs and celery; mix well. Gently stir in crabmeat and mix until just combined. Form into 5 crab cakes and place on platter. Refrigerate 30 minutes. (This helps them maintain their shape while cooking.)

2 In a shallow dish, beat remaining egg with a fork. Place remaining ¾ cup breadcrumbs in another shallow dish. Dip crab cakes in egg, then in breadcrumbs, making sure they're completely coated, and place back on platter.

3 In a large skillet over medium heat, heat oil until hot. Place crab cakes in skillet and cook 4 to 6 minutes per side or until golden and heated through in center. Drain on a paper towel-lined platter. Serve immediately.

Tina's Tip: *I have a great homemade sauce for these. To make it, mix together ½ cup mayonnaise, 1 teaspoon Dijon mustard, 1 teaspoon hot sauce, ½ teaspoon lemon juice, and a ¼ teaspoon salt; chill and serve.*

We don't live too far from the Chesapeake Bay. It is a beautiful place for us to visit, especially since one of my older sisters has a boat there. One of the things you're bound to see while vacationing in the area is a wide array of crab shacks. No matter where you go along the coast, you can find delicious, cooked-to-order crab cakes made from fresh blue crab. If you can't make it to the Maryland coast, this recipe is the next best thing!

Brown Sugar Glazed Salmon

Serves 4

4 (6-ounce) salmon fillets

Salt for seasoning

Black pepper for seasoning

¼ cup brown sugar

2 tablespoons soy sauce (regular or low sodium)

1-½ tablespoons Chinese-style hot mustard (see Tip)

1 tablespoon rice wine vinegar

1 Preheat oven to 375 degrees F. Line a rimmed baking sheet with aluminum foil and coat with cooking spray.

2 Place salmon on baking sheet and lightly season with salt and pepper. Cook 10 minutes. Remove salmon from oven and preheat broiler.

3 Meanwhile, in a small saucepan over medium heat, combine brown sugar, soy sauce, mustard, and vinegar; bring to a boil. Mix well and remove from heat.

4 Spoon brown sugar-mustard mixture evenly over each salmon fillet and place on top rack. Broil 2 to 3 minutes or until glaze starts to caramelize and fish flakes easily.

Tina's Tip: *If you're not familiar with Chinese-style hot mustard, it's got a little kick to it and can be found with the other Asian foods in your grocery store.*

As you may know already, I don't love all salmon dishes, but that doesn't mean I haven't cooked up a great salmon dinner for friends before. This is a version that's really popular. And if you're not into salmon either, then make the glaze to spoon over some chicken breasts. It's great on both!

Greek-Style Grouper

Serves 4

½ teaspoon dried oregano

½ teaspoon garlic powder

4 (4-ounce) fresh or frozen grouper fillets, thawed if frozen

1 tablespoon capers

1 cup fresh baby spinach

1 plum tomato, chopped

¼ cup feta cheese crumbles

1 In a small bowl, mix oregano and garlic until well combined. Sprinkle both sides of grouper fillets with seasoning.

2 Coat a large nonstick skillet with cooking spray. Over medium-high heat, sauté grouper fillets 3 minutes; turn fillets over.

3 Evenly top each fillet with capers, spinach, tomato, and cheese; cover and continue to cook 3 minutes or until spinach is wilted and fish flakes easily with a fork.

Tina's Tip: *To make this a meal, cook up a package of orzo and toss it with some butter, a splash of lemon juice, and a little salt and pepper. (See my Tip on page 98.)*

The first time I had grouper was in Key West, Florida. It was probably one of the best lunches I've ever had. Since that day, I have prepared grouper a ton of different ways, and this is one of my favorites. It's hard to top a fresh fish dinner that's ready in under 20 minutes. The only thing missing is the oceanfront view and the warm beach breeze.

Fri-Yay
Fish Tacos

Serves 4

1 tablespoon blackened seasoning

1-½ pounds white-fleshed fish fillets, cut into 1-inch pieces (like cod, haddock, or tilapia)

2 tablespoons vegetable oil

8 (6-inch) flour tortillas, warmed

Tangy Coleslaw

2 cups shredded coleslaw mix

2 tablespoons rice wine vinegar

1 tablespoon vegetable oil

Cilantro-Lime Sauce

¼ cup mayonnaise

¼ cup sour cream

2 tablespoons chopped fresh cilantro

2 teaspoons lime juice

¼ teaspoon salt

1 avocado, peeled and diced

1 In a large bowl, sprinkle blackened seasoning over fish and toss until evenly coated.

2 In a large skillet over medium-high heat, heat oil until hot. Cook fish 4 to 5 minutes or until firm, stirring occasionally.

3 Meanwhile, in bowl, combine Tangy Coleslaw ingredients; toss until evenly coated, and set aside.

4 In another small bowl, combine Cilantro-Lime Sauce ingredients; mix well and set aside. (For a creamier sauce, you can place all the ingredients in a blender or chopper and blend until smooth.)

5 Place fish evenly down the center of each tortilla, then top with Tangy Coleslaw and Cilantro-Lime Sauce.

Tina's Tip: *If you prefer to grill your fish, place the whole fillets into a fish basket or on a perforated grill liner and grill over medium-high heat 3 to 4 minutes per side or until firm.*

I like making tacos for the family because they are so customizable. For those of you who love fish tacos, these are a great way to celebrate the end of the week (Fri-yay!) or really any day. I often serve them with pickled red onions (page 44) to give these an extra-tangy kick, but like I said, you could serve them with any of your favorite toppings. Make them your own and have some fun.

Creamy Lemon Shrimp

Serves 4 to 5

2 tablespoons olive oil

⅓ cup finely chopped onion

3 small cloves garlic, minced

½ teaspoon salt

¼ teaspoon black pepper

½ cup dry white wine

1 tablespoon lemon zest

1 tablespoon fresh lemon juice

1 pound large raw shrimp, peeled, deveined, and tails removed

½ cup heavy cream

2 tablespoons chopped fresh parsley or basil

1 pound spaghetti or fettucine, cooked according to package directions (see Tip)

1 In a large skillet over medium heat, heat oil until hot. Add onion, garlic, salt, and pepper. Sauté 3 minutes or until onion is tender, stirring occasionally.

2 Add wine, lemon zest, and lemon juice, and simmer 1 minute. Add shrimp, stir, and continue to cook until shrimp turn pink.

3 Slowly stir in cream and simmer an additional 2 minutes or until sauce thickens and shrimp are cooked through. Stir in parsley and serve immediately over hot pasta.

Tina's Tip: *If you want to go all out, make your own pasta for this recipe. (Check out my recipe on page 142.) And if you really love the fresh taste of lemon, stir in an additional tablespoon of the juice along with the parsley.*

There's just no way to say "no" to this (unless you have to stay away from shellfish). It's creamy, dreamy, and bursting with the bright flavor of fresh lemon and herbs. You can make things a little lighter by serving it over zucchini noodles or another lower-carb veggie noodle.

Three-In-One Homemade Pasta

Makes about 1 pound

2-¼ cups all-purpose flour, plus more as needed

1 tablespoon plus ½ teaspoon salt, divided

3 large eggs

½ teaspoon olive oil

Options:

Spinach Pasta Dough: Puree thawed frozen spinach (do not squeeze dry) in a food processor or blender. Then press pureed spinach into a fine mesh strainer to remove liquid. Measure out 3 tablespoons of spinach puree and add to the egg mixture in the first step. Then, proceed as directed. You may need to add a little more flour to get the desired consistency.

Tomato Pasta Dough: Stir 2-½ tablespoons tomato paste into the egg mixture in the first step and proceed as directed.

1 Using a stand mixer with a dough hook on speed 2, combine flour and salt. In a large measuring cup gently whisk eggs and oil. Slowly drizzle egg mixture into dry ingredients; mix well.

2 Knead dough about 3 to 5 minutes on speed 2 until dough is fairly stiff. (It's okay if it looks a little lumpy.) If your dough becomes very crumbly and isn't coming together, add water, 1 teaspoon at a time. If your dough seems too wet, add flour 1 tablespoon at a time.

3 Wrap dough in plastic wrap and let rest 20 minutes at room temperature or refrigerate overnight.

4 Using a stand mixer with a pasta roller and cutter, cut your favorite shape of pasta. (Refer to your pasta cutter's instructions for more options and additional details.) Drape cut pasta over pasta drying rack, as shown, or lay in single layer on rimmed baking sheets that have been dusted with flour.

5 When ready to cook, bring a large pot of water and remaining 1 tablespoon salt to a boil. Add pasta and cook 2 to 5 minutes or until tender, stirring occasionally. Cooking time will vary depending on thickness of pasta.

When you're married to an Italian, like I am, you've got to know how to make your own pasta. It takes a little more time, but this recipe makes it a lot easier than you think. The results are worth it—homemade pasta always beats the boxed kind.

All-American Mac & Cheese

Serves 10 to 12

1 tablespoon plus ¼ teaspoon salt, divided

1 pound elbow macaroni

6 tablespoons butter

⅓ cup all-purpose flour

¾ teaspoon dry mustard

¼ teaspoon white pepper

4-½ cups milk

½ teaspoon Worcestershire sauce

12 ounces sharp cheddar cheese, shredded

6 ounces deli American cheese, cut into strips

Crispy Crumb Topping

2 tablespoons butter

1 cup panko breadcrumbs

⅛ teaspoon salt

⅛ teaspoon black pepper

1 Preheat oven to 350 degrees F. Coat a 9- x 13-inch baking dish with cooking spray.

2 In a large pot over high heat, bring water and 1 tablespoon salt to a boil. Add macaroni and cook 5 to 6 minutes or until al dente. Drain well and set aside.

3 In the same pot over medium heat, melt 6 tablespoons butter. Stir in the flour, dry mustard, remaining ¼ teaspoon salt, and the white pepper until smooth. Cook 1 to 2 minutes, stirring constantly until it begins to turn golden in color. Whisk ½ cup milk into the butter mixture until smooth. Slowly add remaining 4 cups milk, whisking continually. Heat until sauce thickens, stirring frequently. Before it comes to a boil, remove from heat and stir in Worcestershire sauce and both cheeses, stirring until melted and sauce is smooth.

4 Add macaroni to cheese sauce and stir to combine. Spoon mixture into baking dish. Cover with foil and bake 20 minutes.

5 Meanwhile, to make the Crispy Crumb Topping, in a small microwave-safe bowl, melt 2 tablespoons butter. Stir in the breadcrumbs, salt, and black pepper. Remove baking dish from oven, uncover, and sprinkle with breadcrumb mixture. Continue to bake, uncovered, 20 to 30 minutes or until heated through and top is golden.

Growing up, whenever one of us kids asked what our cultural background was, my mom would always answer, "We're Heinz 57—a little bit of everything." We were raised as a traditional American family and ate a lot of traditional American recipes, like meatloaf and macaroni & cheese. This one is a crowd favorite, made like my Mom used to with a blend of cheeses and a buttery breadcrumb topping.

Chicken Rigatoni with Creamy Marinara

Serves 5 to 6

1 pound rigatoni pasta

3 tablespoons olive oil

1 cup chopped onion

3 cloves garlic, minced

4 boneless, skinless chicken breasts, cut into 1-inch pieces

½ teaspoon salt

½ teaspoon black pepper

¾ cup chicken broth (regular or low sodium)

½ cup white wine

1 cup marinara sauce

3 tablespoons butter

1 cup Parmesan cheese

¼ cup fresh basil, sliced

1 Cook pasta according to package directions; drain.

2 Meanwhile, in a large deep skillet over medium heat, heat oil until hot. Cook onion and garlic 3 to 4 minutes or until tender. Season chicken with salt and pepper, and add to skillet; cook 6 to 8 minutes or until no longer pink.

3 Add broth and wine, and simmer 5 minutes. Stir in marinara sauce and cook 5 minutes. Add butter, Parmesan cheese, and basil, and cook 6 to 8 minutes or until thickened.

4 Slowly stir pasta into skillet, and simmer 5 more minutes or until heated through.

Tina's Tip: *If you like spicy, you can serve this with chopped cherry peppers. They'll complement the flavors of the dish and give it a little kick.*

This is a fun, change-of-pace, weeknight dinner that's perfect for when you're craving something other than your typical spaghetti and meatballs. This super yummy dish is good enough to be served at any restaurant. You might even want to invite your friends and neighbors over for this one. Set out a big green salad and a basket of rolls for the ultimate feast.

Veggie Lover's Lasagna

Serves 6 to 8

3 tablespoons olive oil

1 large yellow bell pepper, chopped

½ cup chopped onion

3 cups chopped fresh broccoli

3 cloves garlic, minced

1 (15-ounce) container ricotta cheese

1 egg

3 cups (12 ounces) shredded mozzarella cheese, divided

½ teaspoon salt

1 (24-ounce) jar marinara sauce

9 uncooked lasagna noodles

1 cup water

1 Preheat oven to 350 degrees F. Coat a 9- x 13-inch baking dish with cooking spray. In a skillet over medium heat, heat oil until hot. Add yellow pepper and onion; sauté 3 minutes. Add broccoli and garlic, and cook 2 more minutes or until vegetables are softened; let cool slightly.

2 In a large bowl, combine ricotta cheese, egg, 2 cups mozzarella cheese, the salt, and the vegetable mixture; mix well.

3 Pour half the marinara sauce into baking dish. Cover sauce with 3 uncooked noodles; spread half of ricotta cheese mixture evenly over noodles. Repeat with 3 more noodles, remaining ricotta mixture, 3 more noodles, and remaining marinara sauce. Pour ¼ cup water into each corner of dish.

4 Cover tightly with aluminum foil and bake 1-¼ hours. (Don't peek while this is cooking. You don't want the steam to escape, since the steam is what makes your noodles nice and tender.)

5 Remove from oven, sprinkle with remaining 1 cup mozzarella cheese, and place back in oven, uncovered, 10 minutes or until cheese is melted. Let rest 10 minutes before serving.

There are a lot of families experimenting with going meatless at least once a week. I know it can be challenging finding new meatless recipes that the whole family will enjoy, which is why I came up with this one. This hearty lasagna is vegetarian-friendly and easily adaptable. (Use veggies your family likes or whatever you have at home.) Plus, it's really easy, so you won't be spending a ton of time in the kitchen assembling it. Just prepare, bake, and enjoy.

Cheesy Sausage Stuffed Shells

Serves 6 to 8

22 to 24 jumbo pasta shells

1 tablespoon olive oil

1 pound turkey sausage, removed from casing if necessary

¼ cup finely chopped onion

3 cloves garlic, minced

1 teaspoon Italian seasoning

½ teaspoon salt

¼ teaspoon black pepper

1 (15-ounce) container ricotta cheese

1 (10-ounce) package frozen chopped spinach, thawed and squeezed dry

¼ cup grated Parmesan cheese

2 cups (8 ounces) shredded mozzarella cheese, divided

1 egg

1 (15-ounce) jar Alfredo sauce

1 Preheat oven to 350 degrees F. Coat a 9- x 13-inch baking dish with cooking spray. Cook shells according to package directions for al dente; drain well.

2 Meanwhile, in a large skillet over medium heat, heat oil until hot. Sauté sausage and onion 5 to 6 minutes or until browned; drain fat. Stir in garlic, Italian seasoning, salt, and pepper and heat 2 minutes; set aside to cool.

3 In a medium bowl, combine ricotta cheese, spinach, Parmesan cheese, 1 cup mozzarella cheese, and the egg; mix well. Add sausage mixture to cheese mixture; mix until well blended.

4 Pour ¾ cup of Alfredo sauce over bottom of baking dish. Stuff shells with sausage/cheese mixture (see Tip) and place in baking dish. Top shells with remaining Alfredo sauce.

5 Cover with foil and bake 35 minutes. Uncover, sprinkle with remaining 1 cup mozzarella cheese, and bake an additional 5 to 7 minutes or until cheese is melted and filling is heated through.

Tina's Tip: *You can stuff the cooked shells using a teaspoon or place the filling in a resealable plastic bag with one corner snipped off and pipe the filling in.*

You can easily feed a crowd or a big family with a large dish of stuffed shells. They're ooey-gooey and packed with flavor, so don't count on having a lot left over—these almost always disappear.

Pesto & Peppers Cheese Tortellini

Serves 4 to 6

Homemade Pesto

2 cups packed fresh basil leaves

¾ cup grated Parmesan cheese

2 small cloves garlic

¼ cup pine nuts

¾ cup olive oil

1 pound cheese tortellini

¼ cup chopped roasted red peppers

Tina's Tip: *To help keep your pesto a bright green color, add a splash of lemon juice along with the olive oil.*

1 To make the Homemade Pesto, place basil, Parmesan cheese, garlic, and pine nuts in a chopper, food processor, or blender. Pulse until mixture is coarsely chopped. Gradually add olive oil and process to desired consistency, scraping bowl as needed; set aside.

2 Cook tortellini according to package directions; drain, and reserve ¼ cup of cooking water.

3 Place hot, cooked tortellini in a serving bowl, along with the reserved cooking water. Add red peppers and desired amount of pesto sauce. (I suggest you start with half and add more until you get it just as saucy as you like.) Toss until evenly coated; serve immediately. Any leftover pesto can be refrigerated for up to 4 to 5 days for later use.

I love pesto and make a ton of it in the summer when I have basil growing outside my kitchen door. It's such a versatile sauce that can be used in everything from sandwiches and chicken to pasta dishes, like this one. Because my whole family loves it, I make this in big batches. (I'll admit it—sometimes I incorporate pesto into 3 to 4 meals a week!)

Supreme Stuffed Portobello Mushrooms

Makes 4

4 large portobello mushrooms (about 3 inches each)

½ cup diced pepperoni

1-½ cups fresh spinach leaves, coarsely chopped

2 tablespoons drained and chopped banana pepper rings

1 cup (4 ounces) shredded mozzarella cheese

⅓ cup Italian breadcrumbs

2 cloves garlic, minced

¼ teaspoon salt

¼ teaspoon black pepper

2 tablespoons olive oil

1 Preheat oven to 375 degrees F. Coat a rimmed baking sheet with cooking spray.

2 Gently clean mushrooms by wiping them with damp paper towels. Remove stems, set aside caps, and coarsely chop stems.

3 In a large bowl, combine chopped mushroom stems, pepperoni, spinach, banana peppers, mozzarella cheese, breadcrumbs, garlic, salt, black pepper, and oil; mix well. Evenly fill each mushroom cap with mixture and place on rimmed baking sheet.

4 Bake 25 to 30 minutes or until heated through and mushroom caps are fork-tender.

Tina's Tip: *Grate on some Parmesan cheese right before serving for extra-cheesy goodness.*

There are so many delicious ways to serve dinner-sized stuffed mushrooms; it was hard to choose just one of the many versions I've made over the years. The combination of ingredients in this one remind me of a supreme pizza! You can make these giant mushrooms for dinner or cut them into quarters and serve them as an appetizer. And if you want to make them vegetarian-friendly, just leave out the pepperoni.

Easy Classic Pizza Dough

Makes enough dough for 1 large or 2 small pizzas

2-½ cups all-purpose flour (additional for rolling/stretching dough) (see Tip)

1 teaspoon salt

1 (.25-ounce) packet instant/rapid rise yeast (2-¼ teaspoons)

3 tablespoons olive oil, divided

¾ cup warm water (approximately 105 degrees F)

Tina's Tip: *You can refrigerate the dough for up to 2 days after it rises. I usually cook my pizzas on a pizza stone in a 475 degree oven or on a grill set to high. You can also use bread flour in place of the all-purpose flour. If you have trouble with your dough springing back when you try to stretch it, let it relax for 5 minutes and try again.*

1 Using a stand mixer with a dough hook on speed 2, combine flour, salt, and yeast. In a measuring cup, combine 2 tablespoons olive oil and the water. Slowly drizzle olive oil mixture into dry ingredients; mix well. Knead dough about 5 minutes or until dough forms a smooth elastic ball. (If you don't have a stand mixer, you can knead the dough by hand. If the dough seems very sticky, you can sprinkle in another teaspoon or two of flour.)

2 With remaining 1 tablespoon oil, grease inside of a medium bowl. Place dough in bowl and turn to coat in oil. Cover with plastic wrap and place in a warm spot to rise until doubled in size, about 1 hour.

3 Gently press down dough to deflate. Form into disc shape and lightly dust with flour. Cover with plastic wrap and let rest on counter 15 minutes.

4 Roll/stretch dough on a lightly floured surface. (If you know how to toss the dough in the air like they do in the movies or at your favorite pizza place, this would be a good time to show off.)

This is such an easy pizza dough to make and roll out—you'll be whipping up homemade pizzas in no time. (How about trying my recipe for Mama Mia's Meatball pizza on the next page?) If I know I want to do a pizza night later in the week, I'll usually make it ahead of time and keep it in the fridge. This dough is also great for making flatbreads and focaccia. Have fun topping with whatever you're in the mood for!

Mama Mia's Meatball Pizza

Serves 4 to 6

1 tablespoon cornmeal

1 (1-pound) pizza dough (see Tip)

¾ cup pizza sauce

1-¼ cups (5 ounces) shredded mozzarella cheese

1 teaspoon Italian seasoning

6 ounces (about 12) frozen meatballs, thawed and cut in half (see note)

½ cup ricotta cheese

2 tablespoons shaved Parmesan cheese

2 tablespoons slivered fresh basil

1 Preheat oven to 475 degrees F. Sprinkle cornmeal on a pizza pan or rimmed baking sheet.

2 Place dough on a lightly floured surface. With a rolling pin, or using your hands, shape dough into a 12- to 14-inch circle. Place dough on pizza pan or baking sheet.

3 Spread sauce evenly over dough; sprinkle with mozzarella cheese and Italian seasoning. Top with meatballs, dollops of ricotta cheese, and Parmesan cheese. Bake 15 to 20 minutes or until crust is crisp and brown. Sprinkle with basil and serve.

Tina's Tip: *My Easy Classic Pizza Dough recipe (on the previous page) is perfect for this, but if you don't have the time to make homemade dough, you can use a refrigerated pizza dough or pick up a ball of dough at your favorite pizza place.*

Using store-bought meatballs makes this super convenient; however, when time permits, I like to make homemade meatballs for this. (See my recipe on page 116.) If you're a fan of meatball subs or meatballs in general, this pizza is right up your alley. I especially love how the dollops of ricotta look like little clouds nestled between the meatball halves. It's like a dream come true.

Fig, Prosciutto, and Arugula Flatbread

Serves 4 to 6

1 (8- to 11-ounce) package refrigerated thin crust pizza dough (see Tip)

⅓ cup fig jam

½ (8-ounce) Brie cheese wheel, cut into thin wedges

½ cup fresh arugula

6 to 8 thin slices prosciutto, cut in half

Balsamic glaze for drizzling

1 Preheat oven to 400 degrees F. Coat a rimmed 10- x 15-inch baking sheet with cooking spray.

2 Unroll dough and place onto baking sheet. Bake 10 minutes or until set.

3 Remove from oven and spread fig jam evenly over crust; top with wedges of brie. Bake 7 to 9 minutes or until crust is crispy and cheese is melty.

4 Remove from oven and top with arugula and prosciutto. Drizzle with balsamic glaze, slice, and serve.

Tina's Tip: *Refrigerated dough is super convenient; however, when time permits, go ahead and make my homemade pizza dough. (See page 153.)*

The great thing about flatbreads is you don't have to worry about making them any specific shape and, just like pizzas, you can top them with any creative combination of ingredients. I wanted you to have something a little fancy that you could serve at a holiday dinner or anytime you have company coming over, which is why I went the fig-jam-and-Brie route. (If you haven't tried fig jam, you are in for a treat!) Serve this with Prosecco and enjoy!

Balsamic Veggie Stacks

Makes 4

Balsamic Vinaigrette

⅓ cup olive oil

3 tablespoons white balsamic vinegar (see Tip)

1 tablespoon Dijon mustard

½ teaspoon dried oregano

¼ teaspoon salt

¼ teaspoon black pepper

1 eggplant, cut into 8 (¼-inch thick) slices

1 zucchini, cut into 12 (¼-inch thick) slices

1 tomato, cut into 4 (¼-inch thick) slices

⅓ cup olive oil

Salt and pepper for sprinkling

1 (8-ounce) ball fresh mozzarella cheese, cut into 8 slices

1 To make Balsamic Vinaigrette, in a small bowl or chopper, combine all ingredients until well mixed; set aside.

2 Preheat oven to 425 degrees F. Arrange eggplant, zucchini, and tomato slices in a single layer on two rimmed baking sheets. Brush veggies on both sides with oil and sprinkle with salt and pepper.

3 Roast 15 minutes; remove tomatoes to a plate. Continue to roast vegetables 15 more minutes or until softened.

4 To assemble the stacks, top half the eggplant slices with a slice of mozzarella, a slice of tomato, 3 slices of zucchini, another slice of mozzarella, and another slice of eggplant.

5 Place baking sheet back in oven and bake 5 more minutes or until cheese is melty. Remove from oven and top each stack with a drizzle of vinaigrette. Serve immediately.

Tina's Tip: *I often make a double batch of this vinaigrette. That way I have it on hand when I'm craving a fresh, homemade dressing. If you'd like, you can use traditional balsamic vinegar or even a flavored balsamic instead of the white balsamic vinegar.*

This is a great recipe to make towards the end of summer when the veggies are fresh and abundant. I love the trio of eggplant, zucchini, and tomato, especially when it's sandwiched with fresh mozzarella. Don't care for eggplant like my husband? Double up on the other veggies. The vinaigrette ties it all together. Enjoy this for lunch or dinner, preferably outside, on a patio, under a warm summer sky.

Sides

Roasted Country Vegetables 162

Bacon-Wrapped Green Bean Bundles 164

Garlic-Parmesan Brussels Sprouts 166

Chili Butter Corn on the Cob 168

Marinated Cucumber Salad 169

Smoky & Sweet Baked Beans 170

Brown Sugar Grilled Pineapple 172

Cheesy Cauliflower and Potato Mash 174

Caprese Orzo Salad 176

Homemade Spaetzle 178

Best-of-Both-Worlds Potato Salad 179

Touch-of-Honey Sweet Potato Mash 180

Not-Your-Everyday Cornbread Stuffing 182

Rosemary Lemon Smashed Potatoes 184

Creamy Risotto Carbonara 186

Cheddar-Stuffed Yeast Rolls 188

Roasted Country Vegetables

Serves 6 to 8

¼ cup olive oil

½ teaspoon dried oregano

½ teaspoon dried thyme

½ teaspoon dried basil

4 cloves garlic, slivered

½ teaspoon kosher salt, plus more to taste

½ teaspoon black pepper

½ large head broccoli, cut into florets

2 red bell peppers, cut into 1-inch chunks

1 onion, cut into 1-inch chunks

1-½ cups baby carrots

1 Preheat oven to 425 degrees F. Coat 2 rimmed baking sheets with cooking spray.

2 In a large bowl, combine oil, oregano, thyme, basil, garlic, salt, and black pepper; mix well. Add vegetables to mixture, tossing until evenly coated. Place on baking sheets.

3 Roast 25 minutes, turn over, and roast 10 more minutes or until tender and edges start to brown.

Tina's Tip: *If you'd like to use fresh herbs, replace the dried herbs with 1 teaspoon each of the fresh, and don't add the fresh basil until the vegetables come out of the oven.*

Everyone in my family enjoys eating roasted vegetables, which is a big change from how some families used to feel about eating their vegetables. If you were born in the 70s or earlier, you know what I'm talking about—there was hardly any appeal to the canned, mushy veggies that were popular in those days. With roasted vegetables, you can actually enjoy the texture. Plus they're so versatile. Eat them as-is or add them to your favorite soups and salads.

Bacon-Wrapped Green Bean Bundles

Makes 6 bundles

8 ounces fresh French green beans, ends trimmed

6 slices thick-cut bacon

Balsamic glaze for drizzling

Coarse black pepper for sprinkling

1 Preheat air fryer to 400 degrees F.

2 Evenly divide green beans into 6 bundles. Wrap each bundle with a slice of bacon, leaving both ends unwrapped (see photo); place in air fryer basket and repeat with remaining green beans and bacon.

3 Air-fry 7 to 9 minutes or until bacon is crisp and green beans are crisp-tender. Drizzle with balsamic glaze and a sprinkle of black pepper.

Tina's Tip: *If you don't have an air fryer, no worries. You can make these in your traditional oven, on a wire rack over a rimmed baking sheet. Simply preheat your oven to 425 degrees and roast for about 20 minutes.*

Here's an easy way to dress up your green beans for company, the holidays, or any time you want to make dinner feel a little more special. (As a bacon lover, I can find just about any excuse to make these.) These bacon-wrapped bundles beat an ordinary pile of green beans any day, and the balsamic glaze (which you can usually find near the other salad dressings and vinegars at your grocery store) adds the perfect sweet and tangy touch.

Garlic-Parmesan Brussels Sprouts

Serves 5 to 6

2 tablespoons olive oil

1 tablespoon butter, melted

¼ teaspoon salt

¼ teaspoon black pepper

2 cloves garlic, slivered

1-½ pounds Brussels sprouts, trimmed and cut in half

⅓ cup panko breadcrumbs

¼ cup grated Parmesan cheese

1 Preheat oven to 400 degrees F. Coat a rimmed baking sheet with cooking spray.

2 In a large bowl, combine olive oil, butter, salt, and pepper; mix well. Add garlic and Brussels sprouts, and toss until evenly coated.

3 In a small bowl, combine breadcrumbs and Parmesan cheese; sprinkle mixture over Brussels sprouts, gently toss, and place on baking sheet. Sprinkle any extra crumb mixture over sprouts.

4 Roast 15 to 20 minutes or until tender and golden brown.

Tina's Tip: *I like using both butter and olive oil because they do different things. The butter adds a rich flavor and the oil helps these crisp up really nicely.*

I don't have a great history with Brussels sprouts. As a child, I used to pass on the "steamed mini Martian heads" (Lol!) and miss out on dessert for refusing to eat them. It wasn't until I tried them several years later, during dinner with friends, that everything changed. As it turns out, Brussels sprouts can be amazing—if you make them the right way. These are full of caramelized yumminess with crispy leaves and a delicious garlicky-Parmesan coating.

Chili Butter
Corn on the Cob

Serves 8

1 stick butter, softened

1 tablespoon chili powder

2 tablespoons chopped
fresh cilantro

1 teaspoon salt

¼ teaspoon black pepper

8 ears fresh corn, husked

2 limes, cut into quarters

1 Preheat grill to medium-high heat.

2 In a small bowl, combine butter, chili powder, cilantro, salt, and pepper; mix well. Brush corn with butter mixture, coating completely. Wrap each ear in a piece of heavy-duty aluminum foil.

3 Place wrapped corn on grill rack and cook 10 to 12 minutes or until kernels are tender, turning halfway through cooking. Carefully open foil, remove corn, squeeze a quarter of lime over each, and serve.

Tina's Tip: *The best way to know if your corn is done is to take one ear off the grill, carefully open the foil, and cut off a few kernels. I like them when they're tender, but still pop in your mouth when you bite into them.*

Our local farmers' market has some of the best Jersey corn, so we go there often to get fresh corn when it's in season. I grill or roast a lot of corn during the summer, not only for barbecues, but also because I love using leftover corn in salads and dips. (See my Street Corn Layer Dip on page 48). In this recipe, the chili butter jazzes up the sweet corn with a little zest.

Marinated Cucumber Salad

Serves 6 to 8

8 cups thinly sliced cucumbers
(about 5 cucumbers)

1 large sweet onion, thinly sliced

½ red bell pepper, chopped

1-½ cups white vinegar

½ cup sugar

2 cloves garlic, finely chopped

1 tablespoon vegetable oil

4 teaspoons salt

1 cup water

½ teaspoon white pepper

3 tablespoons chopped fresh dill

1 In a large bowl, combine cucumbers, onion, and red bell pepper; set aside.

2 In a large saucepan, mix together vinegar, sugar, garlic, oil, salt, and water; bring to a boil, stirring frequently. Let cool slightly, pour over cucumber mixture, add white pepper and dill, and mix well.

3 Refrigerate until chilled, then serve.

Tina's Tip: *The easiest way to get thin slices of cucumber is to use a food processor with a slicing blade. (If you don't have one you might want to put that on next year's list for Santa.) Otherwise, you can use a mandoline or a sharp knife. And if you don't have fresh dill, a teaspoon of dried should do the trick.*

Make this ahead of time so you can have it ready for those days when you want something cool and refreshing—like during the hot summer months. When I was pregnant with my first daughter, Sam, I couldn't get enough of my Mother-in-Law, Evelyn's, version. It's just addictively good!

Smoky & Sweet Baked Beans

Serves 12 to 15

¾ pound bacon, cut in ½-inch pieces

1 large sweet onion, chopped

6 (15.5-ounce) cans navy beans, drained and rinsed

1-¼ cups barbecue sauce

2 (8-ounce) cans tomato sauce

1 cup beer

3 tablespoons brown sugar

¼ cup molasses

2 tablespoons Dijon mustard

2 tablespoons Worcestershire sauce

1 tablespoon soy sauce

5 teaspoons smoked paprika

2 tablespoons cider vinegar

1 Preheat oven to 350 degrees F. Coat a 9- x 13-inch baking dish with cooking spray.

2 In a large skillet over medium heat, cook bacon until crispy. Remove to a paper towel-lined plate and pour off all but 2 tablespoons of pan drippings. Add onion to skillet and cook 5 minutes.

3 In a large bowl, add beans, onion, bacon, and remaining ingredients. Stir to combine and pour into baking dish.

4 Bake 1 to 1-¼ hours or until bubbly and heated through in center.

Tina's Tip: *If you prefer, you can make these in a slow cooker. After step 2, mix everything in your slow cooker and cook on HIGH 3 hours or LOW 6 to 7 hours. You can also freeze these for later. If I'm not cooking for a crowd, I'll divide up the batch and freeze in smaller containers. Then when I want baked beans, I just thaw and reheat in the microwave. Don't have navy beans? Great Northern beans are a great substitute.*

I spent an entire summer perfecting this recipe. I finally got them just the way I like them—saucy, a little smoky, a bit sweet, and loaded with bacon! I love to pile them on hot dogs (and even secretly eat them in toasted cheese sandwiches). I never cared much for baked beans when I was younger, but now I'm a big fan!

Brown Sugar Grilled Pineapple

Serves 8

1 fresh pineapple, cored and peeled

½ cup teriyaki sauce

¼ cup brown sugar

1 tablespoon vegetable oil

1 Preheat grill to medium. Cut pineapple, crosswise, into 8 slices.

2 In a 9- x 13-inch baking dish, combine teriyaki sauce, sugar, and oil; mix well.

3 Add pineapple and turn until evenly coated. Let stand 15 minutes, turning pineapple once. Remove pineapple from marinade; discard marinade.

4 Place pineapple on grill and cook 2 to 3 minutes per side or until pineapple has caramelized.

Tina's Tip.: *To keep things exciting, I like to make these a little differently each time. Sometimes I drizzle the pineapple slices with honey after they cook, and other times I add a little rum or a sprinkle of cinnamon sugar.*

Fresh pineapple is great the way it is, but if you haven't tried it grilled, you're missing out. Grilling pineapple makes it tender and juicier. It's also a great side dish to any of your spring or summer entrees. Pair it with my Roasted Pork with Pineapple-Pepper Jelly on page 114 for double the pineapple goodness. This brings back great memories of our honeymoon in Hawaii!

Cheesy Cauliflower and Potato Mash

Serves 8 to 10

2-½ cups milk

1-¼ teaspoons salt

½ teaspoon black pepper

2 pounds Yukon Gold potatoes, peeled and cut into 1-inch cubes (about 5 cups)

2 medium cloves garlic, peeled

5 cups fresh cauliflower florets

3 tablespoons butter

2 cups shredded cheddar cheese, divided

2 tablespoons sliced chives or scallions, plus more for topping

2 eggs, lightly beaten

1 Preheat oven to 350 degrees F. Coat a 1-½-quart casserole dish with cooking spray.

2 In a large pot over medium-high heat, add milk, salt, pepper, potatoes, garlic, and cauliflower. (Make sure potatoes are below the cauliflower, so that they can cook nice and tender.) Partially cover and bring to a boil, then reduce heat to low. Simmer 15 to 20 minutes or until potatoes and cauliflower are very tender.

3 Remove pan from heat and mash using a hand mixer or immersion blender. Stir in butter and 1-¼ cup cheese. Stir in the chives and eggs, then pour into casserole dish.

4 Bake 30 minutes, sprinkle with remaining ¾ cup cheese, and bake an additional 10 minutes or until edges are golden brown and cheese is melted. Top with additional chives, if desired.

Tina's Tip: *This can be prepared ahead of time, refrigerated, and baked the next day. If you do that, make sure you bake it until it's heated through, which will take an additional 20 minutes or so. (I suggest covering it for the first 30 minutes, so the top doesn't get too brown.) Just make sure you don't forget to add the remaining cheese at the end as indicated above.*

I like to test recipes when there are extra people around. So I made this when my husband had band practice at our house. Everyone loved it, including the non-cauliflower eaters. I like that it's a healthy compromise—you get the yummy taste you love from mashed potatoes, but with fewer carbs.

Caprese Orzo Salad

Serves 4 to 6

Red Wine Vinaigrette

½ cup olive oil

3 tablespoons red wine vinegar

1 tablespoon honey

1 small clove garlic, minced

1 teaspoon salt

¼ teaspoon black pepper

8 ounces orzo pasta, cooked according to package directions and rinsed

1 cup grape tomatoes, cut in half

8 ounces fresh mozzarella pearls (see Tip)

¼ cup thinly sliced fresh basil

1 To make Red Wine Vinaigrette, in a medium bowl, whisk oil, vinegar, honey, garlic, salt, and pepper; set aside. (Or you can mix it all in a chopper.)

2 In a large bowl, combine orzo, tomatoes, mozzarella, and basil. Pour vinaigrette over orzo mixture and toss gently until combined. Serve immediately or cover and chill until ready to serve.

Tina's Tip: *Mozzarella pearls are smaller than mini mozzarella balls. If you're having a hard time finding them, just buy the mini balls and cut them in half. Also, if you're not serving this salad right away, I suggest adding the fresh basil right before you do. Nothing beats the aroma of fresh basil.*

We love pasta salad at our house. It's the perfect side dish at barbecues and picnics. Every time I make this one, I dream about making my own mozzarella cheese someday. Whenever I do get around to it, you can bet I'll be sharing it on my blog, *epicuricloud.com*. It's one of those things on my cooking bucket list!

Homemade Spaetzle

Serves 4 to 5

2 cups all-purpose flour

1 teaspoon salt

Pinch nutmeg

2 large eggs

¾ cup water

3 tablespoons butter

¼ teaspoon black pepper

1 tablespoon sliced chives

1 tablespoon chopped parsley

1 Bring a large pot of salted water to a rolling boil over high heat.

2 In a large bowl, whisk together flour, salt, and nutmeg. In a small bowl, whisk eggs with water. Stir wet ingredients into dry. (The mixture should be the texture of a thick pancake batter. Add an additional tablespoon of water if the batter seems too thick.)

3 With a slotted spoon, scoop up some of the mixture. Use a spatula to press the batter through the slots into the hot water. (See Tip.) Cook 3 to 4 minutes, stirring frequently. When the spaetzle float to the top of the water, remove with a clean slotted spoon. Repeat with any remaining batter.

4 In a large skillet over medium-low heat, melt butter. Add spaetzle and pepper, and cook 4 to 5 minutes or until heated through. Sprinkle with chives and parsley, and serve immediately.

Tina's Tip: *I know the whole idea of dropping batter into hot water through a slotted spoon might seem strange, but it works great. The key is to make sure the slots on whatever you use aren't too big or small. It should allow the batter to bead as it enters the boiling water. If you prefer, you can buy special spaetzle tools to make your experience even more authentic.*

Spaetzle (pronounced "shpet' zul" or "shpet' zlee") is a cross between a noodle and a dumpling. I have German ancestors on both sides of my family, and although I didn't eat a lot of German food growing up, whenever I make this I feel like it's connecting me to my roots. My youngest daughter, Lauren, absolutely loves this side dish!

Best-of-Both-Worlds Potato Salad

Serves 8 to 10

3 pounds small red potatoes

1 tablespoon plus 1-½ teaspoons salt, divided

⅓ cup apple cider vinegar

1 tablespoon Dijon mustard

¾ teaspoon black pepper

1 cup light mayonnaise

3 hard-boiled eggs, chopped

⅓ cup sliced scallions

1 cup sliced celery

1 Place potatoes in a large pot and add enough water to cover them. Stir in 1 tablespoon salt. Bring to boil over high heat. Once boiling, reduce heat to medium and cook 20 to 25 minutes or until fork-tender. Drain and cool slightly.

2 In a large bowl, combine vinegar, mustard, remaining 1-½ teaspoons salt, and the pepper. Cut potatoes into 1-inch chunks and toss with vinegar mixture. Let stand about 30 minutes to absorb the flavors.

3 Add mayonnaise, eggs, scallions, and celery and toss to coat.

Tina's Tip: *The key to making really good potato salad is to toss the dressing mixture over the potatoes while the potatoes are still warm. That allows the potatoes to absorb all the flavors.*

Two people in my life make really great potato salad! Cathy, my next-door neighbor and friend, makes a wonderful red bliss potato salad with apple cider vinegar and scallions. My sister, Nancy, makes hers with mustard and hard-boiled eggs. I decided my recipe should include ingredients I love from both of their recipes.

Touch-of-Honey Sweet Potato Mash

Serves 6 to 8

4 pounds sweet potatoes, peeled, cut into chunks

3-½ teaspoons salt, divided

6 tablespoons butter, softened

¼ cup honey

½ teaspoon cinnamon

½ teaspoon orange zest

¼ teaspoon black pepper

1 Place sweet potatoes in a large pot and add just enough water to cover. Add 2 teaspoons salt to water. Bring to a boil over high heat. Once boiling, reduce heat to medium and simmer 20 to 25 minutes or until potatoes are just tender. Drain well and return potatoes to pot. Place pot back on heat 1 minute, to ensure there's no water left.

2 Add butter, honey, remaining 1-½ teaspoons salt, the cinnamon, orange zest, and pepper. Beat with an electric mixer until smooth and creamy. Serve piping hot.

Tina's Tip: *For an extra bit of sweetness, drizzle a little more honey over the top right before serving.*

My mom, Pat, is a great cook and a creative one at that! She made these one year and served portions in hollowed out orange cups. It really wowed us all. If you're a QVC viewer, you've probably seen me make this yummy mash a bunch of times to demo a hand mixer. (Thanks, Mom!) You should know, I haven't met anyone at the studio who doesn't love this sweet and buttery side dish.

Not-Your-Everyday Cornbread Stuffing

Serves 10 to 12

1-½ sticks butter

1 large onion, chopped

6 stalks celery, chopped

2 (1-pound) cornbreads or
2 packages cornbread mix,
prepared according to package
directions, cubed

4 slices stale challah or brioche
bread, cubed

3 tablespoons chopped
fresh sage

2 tablespoons chopped
fresh parsley

2 tablespoons chopped
fresh thyme

2 teaspoons salt

1 teaspoon black pepper

8 slices crispy cooked bacon,
crumbled

3 cups chicken broth
(regular or low sodium)

1 Preheat oven to 350 degrees F. Coat a
9- x 13-inch baking dish with cooking spray.

2 In a skillet over medium heat, melt butter.
Add onion and celery, and sauté 10 to 12 minutes
or until softened.

3 In a large bowl, combine cornbread, challah,
sage, parsley, thyme, salt, and pepper; mix well.
Add onion and celery, cooked bacon, and chicken
broth; toss gently until thoroughly combined.
Spoon into baking dish.

4 Cover and bake 40 minutes. Uncover and bake
an additional 15 to 20 minutes or until heated
through and top is a little crispy.

I have to admit, I don't serve this on Thanksgiving, but that's only because we always
make my Mom's special stuffing for the holidays. However, I do make this at other
times of the year, and I can easily say it would be a great one for the holidays. The
combination of cornbread and challah bread, plus the bacon and all the fresh herbs,
makes this really flavorful and unique. It's a must-try!

Rosemary Lemon Smashed Potatoes

Serves 5 to 6

1-¼ pounds baby red potatoes (about 18)

¼ cup olive oil

Zest of 1 lemon

2 tablespoons lemon juice

2 cloves garlic, minced

1 sprig fresh rosemary, leaves removed, chopped, and stems discarded

½ teaspoon salt

¼ teaspoon black pepper

1 Place potatoes in a large pot and add just enough water to cover; bring to a boil over high heat. Reduce heat to medium and simmer 20 to 25 minutes or until potatoes are just tender; drain and let cool slightly.

2 Preheat oven to 450 degrees F. Coat a rimmed baking sheet with cooking spray. Place potatoes on baking sheet. Using a large spoon or the bottom of a drinking glass, gently press down on each potato to smash it so it ends up about ½-inch thick (see photo). Make sure you keep the potato as one piece.

3 In a small bowl, combine oil, lemon zest, lemon juice, garlic, rosemary, salt, and pepper; mix well. Brush half the mixture on top of potatoes.

4 Roast 15 minutes or until bottoms begin to brown. Gently flip potatoes and brush with remaining oil mixture. Roast 12 to 15 minutes more or until both sides are browned and crispy; serve hot.

Tina's Tip: *You can boil the potatoes a day or two ahead, and then smash and season them right before roasting.*

It's not too often that you get to smash your food as an adult, so these are pretty fun to make. And because they're smashed, more of the potato gets crispy (which everyone knows—the best part of roasted potatoes are the crispy pieces!). These are really versatile and can be served alongside anything from meatloaf and pork chops to a roasted chicken dinner.

Creamy Risotto Carbonara

Serves 4 to 6

3-½ cups chicken broth (regular or low-sodium)

5 tablespoons butter, divided

½ cup finely chopped onion

1 cup uncooked Arborio rice

1 teaspoon minced garlic

½ cup grated Parmesan cheese

2 slices crispy cooked bacon, crumbled

¼ teaspoon black pepper

½ cup frozen peas, thawed

1 In a medium saucepan over medium heat, bring chicken broth to a simmer; do not let boil. Reduce heat to low and keep warm.

2 Meanwhile, in a large saucepan over medium-high heat, melt 4 tablespoons butter. Add the onion and sauté 4 to 5 minutes or until tender. Stir in rice and garlic; sauté 1 minute.

3 Add ½ cup broth; cook until liquid is absorbed. Add 1 cup broth, stirring constantly until liquid is nearly absorbed. Repeat process, adding remaining broth 1 cup at a time, and stirring constantly until each addition of broth is absorbed before adding the next cup. (This will take about 15 minutes. Don't rush this step—it's what makes the risotto really good!)

4 Remove from heat. Stir in remaining 1 tablespoon butter, the Parmesan cheese, bacon, pepper, and peas. Serve immediately.

Some people think risotto is too intimidating and never give it a try. My version is super easy and super tasty. Just follow the instructions and, before you know it, you'll be a pro. The results are worth it—this risotto is savory, creamy, and so indulgent. You will want to share it with everyone.

Cheddar-Stuffed Yeast Rolls

Makes 12

½ cup milk

¼ cup water

2 tablespoons butter

2 cups all-purpose flour

1 (.25-ounce) envelope or 2-¼ teaspoons instant/rapid rise yeast

1 tablespoon sugar

1 teaspoon Italian seasoning

¼ teaspoon garlic powder

¾ teaspoon salt

12 (¾-inch) cubes cheddar cheese

1 egg

2 teaspoons water

Shredded cheddar cheese

If you've never worked with yeast dough, this is a great recipe to introduce yourself to it. It's worth the extra bit of time it takes. Not only are they fluffy, but they ooze lots of yummy cheddar cheese. They're perfect for dunking in soups and chili or eating them warm out of the oven as-is.

1 In a saucepan over medium heat, heat milk, water, and butter 3 to 5 minutes or until it just begins to simmer; remove from heat and let cool about 2 minutes. In a stand mixer, using a dough hook attachment, combine flour, yeast, sugar, Italian seasoning, garlic powder, and salt. With unit running, add warmed milk mixture to flour mixture and knead on speed 2, 2 to 5 minutes or until dough is smooth and elastic. (If mixture is very wet and sticky add another tablespoon or 2 of flour, but use as little as possible.)

2 For the first rise of dough, use a little oil to coat the inside of a large bowl. Place ball of dough into oil, then turn over so oiled side is upwards. Cover bowl with plastic wrap or a clean kitchen towel and place in a warm spot (80 degrees or so) to rise. Once it's doubled in size (20 to 60 minutes), it's risen enough. Coat an 8-inch round or square pan with cooking spray.

3 Gently press down dough in bowl. Divide dough into 12 portions. Form each piece into a rounded ball, then flatten slightly. Place a cube of cheese in center of dough. Pull up edges of dough around cheese and pinch to seal. Arrange sealed-side down in prepared pan.

4 For the second rise of dough, cover with plastic wrap or a clean towel and place in a warm spot about 30 minutes or until doubled in size, warm, and puffy.

5 Meanwhile, preheat oven to 375 degrees F. Whisk together egg and water and brush on rolls; sprinkle with shredded cheddar cheese. Place pan on lower-middle rack in oven and bake 20 minutes or until golden brown.

Dessert

Mattison Avenue Toffee Cheesecake 192

Fluffy & Creamy No-Bake Cheesecake 194

Cream Cheese Pound Cake 195

Chocolate Layer Birthday Cake 196

Strawberry-Lemon Poke Cake 198

Fudge-Filled Ice Cream Cupcakes 200

Black Forest Dump Cake 202

Salted Pecan Pie Bars 204

My Mom's Homemade Brownies 205

Chocolate Chip & Raspberry Brownies 206

Peanut Butter S'mores Cookie Bars 208

Chocolate-Covered Cookie Butter Balls 210

Triple Chocolate Biscotti 211

White Chocolate Chip Peanut Butter Cookies 212

Cinnamon Crumble Apple Pie 214

My Perfect Pie Crust Dough 215

Peachy Blueberry Crisp 216

Cherry Cobbler with Orange & Almonds 217

Shortbread Cookie Banana Pudding 218

From-Scratch Sweet Dough 220

Party-Time Beignets 221

No-Churn Cookies & Cream Ice Cream 222

Homemade Buttercream Frosting 224

Cream Cheese Frosting 224

Make-Ahead Whipped Cream 225

Sweet & Salty Snack Mix 226

Mattison Avenue Toffee Cheesecake

Serves 12 to 15

24 chocolate sandwich cookies

½ stick butter, melted

3 (8-ounce) packages cream cheese, softened

1 cup sugar

4 large eggs

1 cup sour cream

1 tablespoon cornstarch

1 teaspoon vanilla

1-½ cups chopped toffee candy bars, divided (like Heath® or Skor®)

6 to 8 cups hot water

Chocolate Ganache

1 cup semi-sweet chocolate chips

½ cup heavy cream

When I was teaching at Mattison Avenue Elementary School in the 90s, I was known for my homemade toffee bar cookies. They were loved by all and had an unforgettable taste. While the school's been closed for several years now, and I haven't made these in some time, the memories of them still linger. This recipe is the cheesecake version of those cookies, and it's ready to "make the grade" with your family.

1 Lightly spray a 9-inch springform pan with cooking spray. Place cookies in a food processor and pulse into fine crumbs. In a medium bowl, combine cookie crumbs and butter; mix well. Press mixture into bottom of pan; set aside. (See tip on page viii.)

2 In a large bowl with an electric mixer on medium speed, beat cream cheese and sugar until light and fluffy. Add eggs, sour cream, cornstarch, and vanilla; mix well. Stir in 1 cup chopped candies. Pour mixture into crust.

3 Preheat oven to 425 degrees F. Cut 2 pieces of heavy duty aluminum foil, each 18-inches long, and crisscross them on the counter. Lay pan in center of foil and fold foil up around pan. (This will ensure no water seeps into the pan.) Place pan into roasting pan and put in oven. Gently pour hot water around springform pan, about halfway up, making sure not to splash onto cheesecake.

4 Bake 15 minutes; reduce oven to 200 degrees and bake an additional 1 hour. Turn oven off and allow cheesecake to cool in oven, with door slightly ajar, for 2 hours. Remove from oven, take cheesecake out of water bath, and remove foil. Run a knife around edge of cheesecake and refrigerate, uncovered, until chilled. Cover with plastic wrap and refrigerate 6 hours or overnight. Remove cheesecake from pan and place on a serving platter.

5 To make Chocolate Ganache, place chocolate chips in a medium bowl. In a small saucepan over medium heat, bring heavy cream to a boil, stirring constantly. Pour over chocolate chips, let sit 2 minutes, then stir until mixture is smooth and thickened. Pour ganache over cheesecake and spread over top, allowing some to drip over edge. Chill 20 minutes or until ganache is set. Garnish with remaining ½ cup chopped candies.

Fluffy & Creamy No-Bake Cheesecake

Serves 8 to 10

2 cups graham cracker crumbs (see Tip)

¾ cup sugar, divided

1 stick butter, melted

1 cup heavy cream (whipping cream)

1 tablespoon instant vanilla pudding mix

2 (8-ounce) packages cream cheese, at room temperature

¼ cup sour cream, at room temperature

1-½ teaspoons vanilla

1 In a medium bowl, stir together graham cracker crumbs, ¼ cup sugar, and the butter. Press crust firmly into a 9-inch deep-dish pie plate and refrigerate. (See Tip.)

2 In a large bowl with an electric mixer on medium speed, whip heavy cream and pudding mix until stiff peaks form; set aside.

3 In another bowl, beat cream cheese and remaining ½ cup sugar until creamy. Add in sour cream and vanilla. Continue to beat until well combined, scraping down bowl as needed.

4 Using a spatula, gently fold whipped cream mixture into cream cheese mixture; spoon into chilled crust. Smooth top and refrigerate 8 hours or overnight.

Tina's Tip: *For the crust, you can also use caramelized biscuit cookies (also called speculoos cookies, see page 210). If you happen to have an 8- or 9-inch springform pan, you can use that in place of the pie plate. It's a little easier to remove the slices.*

I love all kinds of cheesecakes, and this one is a true summertime favorite (because there's no need to turn on the oven!). As the name implies, it's a light and creamy cheesecake that pairs perfectly with fresh berries. Just wait till you experience that first scrumptious bite!

Cream Cheese Pound Cake

Makes 2 loaves

2 sticks butter

1 (8-ounce) package cream cheese

2-¾ cups sugar

1 teaspoon kosher salt

6 large eggs

4 teaspoons vanilla

2-⅔ cups all-purpose flour

1 Let butter, cream cheese, and eggs sit out for 30 minutes. Coat 2 (8- x 4-inch) loaf pans with cooking spray and lightly flour. Using an electric mixer on low speed, beat butter about 2 minutes.

2 Add cream cheese and beat on low until well blended. Slowly add sugar and salt. Continue creaming mixture for 5 minutes, scraping bowl halfway through. Increase speed to medium; continue mixing an additional 2 minutes, scraping down bowl as needed.

3 Add eggs, one at a time, beating after each addition, until each egg is fully incorporated. Add vanilla along with the last egg. On low speed, slowly add flour until well blended.

4 Pour batter into pans. Gently tap pans on counter to level out batter and eliminate any air bubbles.

5 Place pans on center rack of cold oven. Turn oven to 300 degrees F. Bake 1-¼ to 1-½ hours, or until a toothpick inserted in center comes out clean. Transfer to wire racks. Cool 10 minutes before removing from pans. Let cool completely before serving.

When you make a pound cake this rich and tasty, you just have to share it. That's why I always make enough for two loaves—one to keep at home and one to share with a friend, neighbor, or loved one. The cream cheese is what really makes this pound cake so incredible. And when it comes to serving, spoon on some berries and whipped cream for even more unbelievable goodness.

Chocolate Layer Birthday Cake

Serves 10 to 12

1 cup cocoa powder, plus extra for dusting

2 cups all-purpose flour

1-¼ teaspoons baking soda

1 teaspoon instant espresso powder (optional)

½ teaspoon baking powder

¼ teaspoon salt

1-½ sticks butter, softened

1-½ cups granulated sugar

3 large eggs

1 cup sour cream

1 teaspoon vanilla

1 cup water

Marshmallow Frosting

2 sticks butter, softened

1 cup marshmallow creme

1 teaspoon vanilla

4 cups powdered sugar

1 Preheat oven to 350 degrees F. Coat 2 (9-inch) cake pans with cooking spray and lightly dust with cocoa powder. In a medium bowl, mix flour, remaining 1 cup cocoa powder, the baking soda, espresso powder, if desired, baking powder, and salt; set aside.

2 In a large bowl using an electric mixer on medium speed, cream butter and sugar for several minutes or until fluffy and lighter in color. Beat in eggs, sour cream, and vanilla until combined. Slowly add dry mixture and water to creamy mixture and beat just until blended.

3 Pour batter evenly into cake pans and bake 30 to 32 minutes or until a toothpick inserted in center comes out clean. Let cool in pans 10 minutes, then remove to a wire rack to cool completely.

4 Meanwhile, to make Marshmallow Frosting, in a large bowl with an electric mixer, beat butter, marshmallow creme, and vanilla until creamy. Slowly add powdered sugar and beat until smooth. Place one cake on a platter, flat-side up, and ice the top with frosting.

5 Place second layer on top and ice the entire cake with remaining frosting. Chill, slice, and enjoy.

You can't have a birthday celebration without cake. And if it's my birthday you're celebrating (woohoo!), then this is my cake of choice. Everything about it is just perfect. Make this for all of the chocolate and vanilla lovers in your life and you can pretty much ensure a happy birthday.

Strawberry-Lemon Poke Cake

Serves 12 to 15

1 package lemon cake mix

2 pounds strawberries,
(1-½ pounds pureed, plus
the remaining sliced thinly)

½ cup sugar

1 teaspoon vanilla

1 (12-ounce) container frozen
whipped topping, thawed
(see Tip)

Tina's Tip: *If you want to make homemade whipped cream, see my recipe on page 225.*

1 Prepare cake mix according to package directions for a 9- x 13-inch baking dish. Bake according to package directions; let cool 10 to 15 minutes.

2 Meanwhile, in a large saucepan over medium heat, add pureed strawberries, sugar, and vanilla. Bring to a boil, stirring continuously. Boil 1 minute, then remove from heat.

3 Using a straw or wooden spoon handle, poke holes randomly into cooled cake. Slowly pour strawberry sauce over cake and into holes, using a spatula to spread. Cover and refrigerate 1 hour or until completely cooled.

4 Evenly spread whipped topping onto cake and refrigerate until ready to serve. Right before serving, top with sliced strawberries.

This cake is so easy to make, thanks to a cake mix shortcut! It features one of my favorite summer flavor combinations—strawberries and lemon—and it's perfect for sharing with friends at any get-together. You can easily make it a day ahead and just pretty it up with the sliced strawberries right before you're ready to take it with you. Every bite tastes like a sweet summer day.

Fudge-Filled Ice Cream Cupcakes

Makes 24 cupcakes

1 package vanilla cake mix

2 cups melted vanilla bean ice cream

3 large eggs

1 (12.8-ounce) jar hot fudge topping

Whipped Cream Frosting

⅓ cup powdered sugar

2 tablespoons vanilla instant pudding mix

1 teaspoon vanilla

2 cups heavy whipping cream

Colorful sprinkles for garnish

1 Preheat oven to 350 degrees F. Place 24 paper liners into cupcake tins.

2 In a large bowl with an electric mixer on medium speed, beat cake mix, melted ice cream and eggs 1 to 2 minutes or until smooth. Pour batter into cupcake liners about ⅔ full. Bake 14 to 16 minutes or until a toothpick inserted comes out clean; let cool.

3 Using an apple corer or paring knife, cut a hole in center of each cupcake, being sure not to cut all the way through to the bottom; remove center. Place hot fudge in a pastry bag or large resealable plastic bag with one corner snipped off. Fill cupcake holes evenly with fudge.

4 To make the Whipped Cream Frosting, in a chilled large bowl with an electric mixer on high speed, beat powdered sugar, instant pudding mix, vanilla, and whipping cream until stiff peaks form.

5 Pipe or spread frosting onto cupcakes and garnish with sprinkles. Refrigerate cupcakes until ready to serve.

Tina's Tip: *Get creative with different flavor combinations. Take any flavor cake mix and any flavor ice cream to make your own custom cupcakes. How about chocolate cake mix with chocolate ice cream for triple the chocolatey goodness?*

You can always count on there being ice cream and cake at any family birthday in my house. This perfect pairing of desserts is what led me to make this all-in-one treat. Now they sort of remind me of little ice cream sundaes, especially with their fudgy centers and colorful sprinkle topping. They're as delicious as they are cute!

Black Forest Dump Cake

Serves 12 to 15

1 package chocolate cake mix

1 (21-ounce) can original cherry pie filling

3 large eggs

1 teaspoon vanilla

Cream Cheese Frosting

1 (8-ounce) package cream cheese, softened

½ stick butter, softened

½ teaspoon vanilla

1 teaspoon milk, plus more if needed

6 cups powdered sugar

Tina's Tip: *Garnish your cake with fresh cherries and chocolate shavings for a classic German look. This frosting recipe makes a generous amount. You can keep any extra in the fridge for a few weeks.*

1 Preheat oven to 350 degrees F. Coat a 9- x 13-inch baking dish with cooking spray.

2 In a large bowl, stir together cake mix, pie filling, eggs, and 1 teaspoon vanilla. Mix gently until well combined. (You want the batter evenly mixed while still keeping some of the cherries whole. The batter will be thick.) Spoon into baking dish.

3 Bake 30 to 35 minutes or until a toothpick inserted in center comes out clean; let cool.

4 Meanwhile, to make Cream Cheese Frosting, in a large bowl using an electric mixer on medium speed, beat cream cheese and butter until smooth and fluffy. Add ½ teaspoon vanilla, the milk, and gradually add the sugar. If the frosting seems too thick, add a little more milk. Mix until smooth and creamy.

5 Frost cake and refrigerate until ready to serve.

This is one of my most popular demo recipes on QVC. Maybe because you only need 4 ingredients and just one baking pan to make it. (I make a homemade cream cheese frosting because I love adding a little homemade touch.) Chocolate and cherries are a classic and yummy flavor combination—it's definitely one of my favorite go-to cakes.

Salted Pecan Pie Bars

Makes 48

Crust:

2 sticks butter, softened

⅔ cup packed light brown sugar

2-⅔ cups all-purpose flour

½ teaspoon salt

Pecan Topping

1 stick butter

1 cup packed light brown sugar

½ cup honey

2 tablespoons heavy cream

½ teaspoon salt, divided

1 teaspoon vanilla

2 cups chopped pecans

1 Preheat oven to 350 degrees F. Coat a 9- x 13-inch baking dish with cooking spray. Line with 2 layers of foil widthwise (enough to hang over the sides of the pan by 2 inches). Coat foil with cooking spray.

2 To make the Crust, in a large bowl with an electric mixer on medium speed, cream 2 sticks butter and ⅔ cups brown sugar 2 to 3 minutes, until light and fluffy. Slowly mix in flour and ½ teaspoon salt. (The mixture will be crumbly.) Press into baking dish. Bake 20 minutes.

3 Meanwhile, to prepare Pecan Topping, in a saucepan over medium-low heat, melt 1 stick butter. Add 1 cup brown sugar, the honey, heavy cream, and ¼ teaspoon salt. Increase heat to medium and bring to simmer, stirring frequently; simmer 1 minute. Stir in vanilla and pecans.

4 Pour the topping over the crust and spread evenly. Return to oven and bake 20 more minutes.

5 Remove from oven and sprinkle with remaining ¼ teaspoon salt while still hot. Allow to cool, then remove from pan using the foil flaps. Remove foil and cut into 48 bite-sized bars. Store in an airtight container.

DESSERT

204

These bars have become a must-have on my Thanksgiving dessert table. From the buttery-rich crust to the salted pecan topping, they're hard to resist. I cut them into small pieces because they're so decadent. At our house, my daughters, my sister, Nancy, and I have a knack for making these disappear rather quickly...

My Mom's Homemade Brownies

Makes 15

4 ounces unsweetened baking chocolate

⅔ cup butter

4 large eggs

2 teaspoons vanilla

2 cups sugar

1-⅓ cups all-purpose flour

½ teaspoon salt

1 teaspoon baking powder

⅔ cup mini chocolate chips

1 Preheat oven to 350 degrees F. Coat a 9- x 13-inch baking dish with cooking spray. (See Tip.)

2 In a small saucepan over low heat, melt chocolate and butter, then remove from heat.

3 In a large bowl, whisk together eggs, vanilla, and sugar. In a medium bowl, stir together flour, salt, and baking powder. Add dry ingredients to egg mixture and stir to combine. Stir in melted chocolate mixture and chocolate chips. Pour batter into baking dish.

4 Bake 30 minutes or until edges are set and center is no longer jiggly. A toothpick inserted should have a few moist crumbs.

Tina's Tip: *To easily remove brownies from baking dish, line the dish with a foil sling. Lay 2 pieces of foil widthwise in dish (enough to hang over the sides by 2 inches). Coat the baking dish and foil with cooking spray. When brownies are cool, use the foil sling to remove them to a cutting board; remove foil before cutting.*

This is my mom's brownie recipe and one of the first recipes I ever baked! According to my mom, I've been baking these since I was about 7 or 8 years old. Even though I've tried plenty of other brownie recipes since then, I always come back to this one. Not only does it bring back such great childhood memories, but it makes the best brownies ever. Thanks, Mom!

Chocolate Chip & Raspberry Brownies

Makes 15

1 package brownie mix
¾ cup chocolate chips
¾ cup raspberry preserves
Powdered sugar for sprinkling

1 Preheat oven to 350 degrees F. Coat a 9- x 13-inch baking dish with cooking spray. Line with 2 layers of foil widthwise (enough to hang over the sides of the pan by 2 inches). Coat foil with cooking spray.

2 Prepare brownie batter according to package directions, but do not bake it yet. Stir in chocolate chips and raspberry preserves. Spread evenly into baking dish.

3 Bake 25 to 30 minutes or until a toothpick inserted has a few moist crumbs.

4 Let cool before cutting. Sprinkle with powdered sugar and serve.

Tina's Tip: *To give these a fancy flair, drizzle each plate with some raspberry ice cream topping. Place a brownie on top of the topping and garnish with fresh raspberries and mint leaves.*

It's amazing what adding just a few special touches to your favorite brownie mix can do! This is a great recipe for those days when you don't have the time to make brownies from scratch, but still want to treat your friends and family to a delicious dessert. It's quick, easy, and sweet enough to make for any special day including Valentine's Day, Christmas, or a birthday.

Peanut Butter S'mores Cookie Bars

Makes 24

1-¾ cups all-purpose flour

1-¾ cups graham cracker crumbs

1 teaspoon baking powder

¼ teaspoon salt

2 sticks butter softened

1-½ cups packed light brown sugar

2 large eggs

2 teaspoons vanilla

1 cup plus 2 tablespoons chocolate chips, divided

¼ cup plus 2 tablespoons peanut butter chips, divided

1-⅓ cups mini marshmallows

Tina's Tip: *If you have an electric knife, this would be a great time to pull it out. It helps you get nice, clean slices!*

1 Preheat oven to 350 degrees F. Coat a 9- x 13-inch metal baking pan with cooking spray. Line with 2 layers of foil widthwise (enough to hang over the sides of the pan by 2 inches). Coat foil with cooking spray.

2 In a large bowl, combine flour, graham cracker crumbs, baking powder, and salt. In another large bowl with an electric mixer on medium speed, cream butter and sugar until light and fluffy. Add eggs one at a time to the butter mixture, then add vanilla. Slowly mix in dry ingredients until just combined.

3 Stir in 1 cup of chocolate chips and ¼ cup peanut butter chips. Press dough into pan. (I use buttered fingers or a spatula.)

4 Bake 25 to 30 minutes or until edges are golden and center is still a little soft. Remove pan from oven, set oven to broil. Sprinkle bars with marshmallows and remaining 2 tablespoons each chocolate and peanut butter chips. Return pan to oven and broil until marshmallows are toasted. (Keep a close watch on these...the marshmallows will toast quickly!)

5 Remove pan from oven and allow to cool completely. Using foil sling, remove to a cutting board. Remove foil and cut into 24 bars. (Wipe knife clean in between cuts to prevent sticking.) Store in an airtight container (but don't pile them up because they'll stick).

S'mores aren't just a summertime campfire dessert. When you add a peanut buttery twist to them, like I do here, they become a year-round treat for my peanut butter-loving girls. (They really like it when I pack one with their lunches.) These are fun to make around Halloween, when you can sprinkle them with Halloween candy (like the candy-coated peanut butter candies). And they freeze really well, individually wrapped, so don't worry about making too many at once.

Chocolate-Covered Cookie Butter Balls

Makes about 50

½ of an (8.8-ounce) package speculoos cookies (such as Biscoff®) (see Tip)

1 (14.1-ounce) jar cookie butter (such as Biscoff®) (see Tip)

1 stick butter

¼ teaspoon salt

½ teaspoon vanilla

2 cups powdered sugar

1 (12-ounce) package semi-sweet chocolate chips

1 tablespoon vegetable shortening

Sprinkles for decorating (optional)

1 Line baking sheets with wax paper. In a food processor, finely crush cookies. Measure 1 cup and set aside.

2 In a large microwave-safe bowl, combine cookie butter, butter, and salt. Microwave 20 to 30 seconds or until ingredients are softened, but not completely melted. Stir in vanilla, crushed cookies, and sugar. Mix well until a dough is formed. Roll mixture into about 50 (1-inch) balls and place on baking sheets. Freeze 20 minutes.

3 Meanwhile, in a microwave-safe bowl, add chocolate chips and shortening, and microwave 60 to 90 seconds or until smooth, stirring occasionally. Be careful not to overheat.

4 Using a toothpick, dip each ball into the melted chocolate, coating evenly. Shake off excess coating and return to baking sheets. Decorate with sprinkles, if desired, and repeat until all balls are coated and decorated. Chill until chocolate is set and enjoy.

Tina's Tip: *Speculoos is a generic name for the traditional, crispy, spiced cookies that originated in Belgium, and can now be found in your grocery store! In recent years, they've become really popular in the U.S. Now they're used to make cookie butter, which has the consistency of peanut butter, but with a sweet cinnamon flavor.*

These cookie balls are inspired by my mother-in-law, Evelyn, who's a wonderful baker. She makes chocolate-covered peanut butter balls which are some of my favorites, so I created my own version that I'm pretty proud of. Plus, they're fun to decorate and give as gifts for different holidays.

Triple Chocolate Biscotti

Makes 48

2-½ cups all-purpose flour

¾ cup unsweetened cocoa powder

1-½ teaspoons baking soda

½ teaspoon salt

5 large eggs

2 cups sugar

1 teaspoon vanilla

1 (10-ounce) package mini semi-sweet chocolate chips

½ cup (3 ounces) white chocolate chips

2 teaspoons vegetable shortening

Tina's Tip: *Looking for a cookie to ship to a friend or loved one? This is it. They're sturdy enough to ship without falling apart, and you can even send along with coffee or a few packets of hot chocolate mix for the perfect drink to dunk them in.*

1 Preheat oven to 350 degrees F. Coat 2 rimmed baking sheets with cooking spray. In a medium bowl, combine flour, cocoa, baking soda, and salt; mix well and set aside.

2 In a large bowl with an electric mixer on medium-high speed, whip or whisk sugar and eggs until light yellow in color, fluffy, and thickened. Stir in vanilla. Using a spatula, gently fold dry ingredients into wet. When lightly mixed, fold in chocolate chips until well mixed. (Dough will be soft, and sticky.)

3 Spoon half the dough evenly down the center (lengthwise) of each baking sheet. With wet hands or a greased spatula, form each mound of dough into a 4- x 12-inch loaf about ¾ inch thick.

4 Bake 30 to 35 minutes or until dough is set, rotating baking sheets halfway through. (The loaves will spread out wider.) Remove from oven and reduce heat to 325 degrees. Allow loaves to cool about 10 minutes before cutting with a large serrated knife into ½-inch-thick slices. Place slices cut-side down on baking sheets and bake an additional 13 to 15 minutes, rotating baking sheets halfway through. Turn slices over and bake another 13 to 15 minutes or until the centers are no longer soft, rotating the sheets again. Allow to cool completely. (The biscotti will firm up even more while cooling.)

5 In microwave-safe container, combine white chocolate chips and shortening. Microwave for 30 second intervals or until melted, stirring each time. Drizzle over one side of the biscotti and allow to cool until the white chocolate firms up. Serve immediately, or store in an airtight container.

White Chocolate Chip Peanut Butter Cookies

Makes 36

1 cup sugar

1 stick butter, softened

1 cup creamy peanut butter

2 large eggs

1 teaspoon vanilla

1-¾ cups all-purpose flour

1 teaspoon baking soda

½ teaspoon salt

1 cup white chocolate chips

1 Preheat oven to 350 degrees F. Lightly coat baking sheets with cooking spray.

2 In a large bowl with an electric mixer on low speed, cream together sugar, butter, and peanut butter. Beat in eggs and vanilla. Add flour, baking soda, and salt; mix just until combined. Stir in white chocolate chips.

3 Drop by heaping teaspoonfuls onto baking sheets. Bake 12 to 14 minutes or until light golden. Cool 10 minutes, then remove to a wire rack to cool completely.

I created these with David Venable in mind (my good friend from "In the Kitchen with David" on QVC) because he just loves peanut butter and white chocolate. One year, I even made him a giant cookie cake with peanut butter and white chocolate. I presented it to him on-air for his birthday and he was so thrilled, I think he might have done the longest happy dance I've ever seen. It's great when I can make a friend feel so special through food.

Cinnamon Crumble Apple Pie

Serves 8

1 single pie crust, homemade (see page 215) or refrigerated (from a 14.1-ounce package

1-¼ cups plus 1 tablespoon all-purpose flour, divided

½ cup light brown sugar

2-¼ teaspoons cinnamon, divided

¼ teaspoon salt

1 stick butter, cubed

⅓ cup quick-cooking oats

2 pounds Granny Smith apples, peeled, cored, and thinly sliced

½ cup granulated sugar

Powdered sugar for dusting

1 Preheat oven to 350 degrees F. Fit pie crust into a 9-inch deep-dish pie plate, pressing crust firmly into plate; flute edges and set aside.

2 In a food processor or chopper, combine 1-¼ cups flour, the brown sugar, 2 teaspoons cinnamon, the salt, and butter. Pulse until crumbs form. Add oats and pulse just until combined.

3 In another large bowl, toss apples with granulated sugar, add remaining 1 tablespoon flour, and remaining ¼ teaspoon cinnamon. Spoon apple mixture into pie crust. Sprinkle crumb mixture over apples, packing lightly. Place pie on baking sheet.

4 Bake 1-¼ hours or until apples are tender and crumbs are golden. If the crumb topping starts to brown too quickly, place a 4-inch square of foil over middle of pie for remaining baking time.

5 Cool on wire rack. Dust with powdered sugar before serving.

Tina's Tip: *I love to use my KitchenAid® spiralizer attachment to quickly peel, core, and slice the apples. I usually bake my pies on the lowest rack of my oven, which ensures the bottom crust gets nice and golden brown, and there's less worry about the top getting too brown.*

Nothing beats a homemade apple pie, and this one has a cinnamon crumb topping that adds both flavor and texture to this classic American dessert. Years ago, we used to go apple picking as a family and bring home baskets of apples for fresh applesauce, pies, and muffins. While we don't do it anymore (we discovered that one of my daughters is allergic to apples) I still like to reminisce and will still bake homemade apple pie, but I make sure to have a separate dessert for Lauren.

My Perfect Pie Crust Dough

Makes enough dough for 2 (9-inch) pie crusts

2-½ cups all-purpose flour, plus more for rolling

1 teaspoon salt

1 tablespoon sugar

6 tablespoons vegetable shortening, cut into 1-inch pieces and chilled

1-½ sticks salted butter, cut into ½-inch cubes and chilled

4 to 6 tablespoons very cold water

Tina's Tip: *I find it's handy to have a shaker with flour in it, to use when dusting your work surface.*

If you have the time, then I suggest making your own pie crust. It's a lot easier than you think and the results are worth it. This makes enough for any recipe that calls for two pie crusts (top and bottom) or you can use just one and freeze the other for the next time there's pie on the menu.

Food Processor Method:

Using the metal blade, pulse to mix dry ingredients. Add shortening and pulse until mixture forms a sandy texture. Add butter and pulse until largest pieces of butter are about pea sized. With unit running, drizzle in water, starting with 4 tablespoons. Stop processor, then continue to add water one tablespoon at a time, pulsing to mix in, until mixture begins to come together, but is still shaggy (not a smooth ball). Repeat until the mixture holds together when pressed.

Stand Mixer Method:

Using a flat beater on low speed, mix dry ingredients. Add shortening and mix on low speed until mixture forms a sandy texture. Add butter and mix until butter is broken down a bit and the largest pieces of butter resemble flattened peas. With mixer on low speed, drizzle in one tablespoon of water. Continue to add water, 1 tablespoon at a time, until mixture comes together. Repeat until the mixture holds together when pressed.

Rolling & Storing Dough:

Dump mixture onto a lightly floured surface and form into a rough ball. Cut in half and press down, creating 2 even discs. (You should still see bits of butter in the dough.) Wrap each disc in plastic wrap and refrigerate 1 hour or overnight. (Dough can also be frozen at this point.) When ready to use, let dough sit 10 minutes, then roll on a floured surface, from center to edge. Turn and dust with flour, as needed, to prevent sticking. Fit into pie plate and repeat with top crust, if using. (If only using 1 crust, place remaining dough into a resealable plastic bag and freeze.) Bake according to your recipe's directions.

Peachy Blueberry Crisp

Serves 6 to 8

Filling:

2-½ cups fresh peaches, pitted, peeled and sliced (about 5 small peaches) (see Tip)

2 cups fresh blueberries

1 teaspoon lemon zest

1 tablespoon lemon juice

⅓ cup granulated sugar

¼ cup all-purpose flour

Crisp Topping:

⅔ cup light brown sugar

½ cup all-purpose flour

5 tablespoons butter, softened

½ teaspoon cinnamon

Pinch of salt

½ cup old-fashioned oats

1 Preheat oven to 350 degrees F.

2 To make the Filling, in a large bowl, stir together all filling ingredients and pour into a 9-inch deep dish pie plate.

3 To make the Crisp Topping, in a food processor or chopper, combine brown sugar, ½ cup flour, the butter, cinnamon, and salt. Pulse until crumbs form. Add oats and pulse until just combined. (Don't over-process the oats.) Sprinkle topping over fruit filling.

4 Place pie plate on a baking sheet and bake 30 minutes or until fruit is bubbly hot and topping is golden.

Tina's Tip: *Since I like my peaches peeled, imagine how excited I was when I discovered a serrated peeler designed to be used with softer foods, like peaches.*

We are big fans of fruit crisp desserts! Actually, of all the baked fruit desserts, anything with a crisp topping is my favorite. They are quick and easy to prepare, and delicious with whatever fruit is in season. I like to serve this warm with real whipped cream or a scoop of vanilla ice cream. It's so good when the buttery topping, juicy fruit, and creamy ice cream start to meld together!

Cherry Cobbler with Orange & Almonds

Serves 6

4 tablespoons butter

1 cup all-purpose flour

1-½ teaspoons baking powder

¼ teaspoon salt

1 cup milk

⅔ cup sugar

1 teaspoon vanilla

2-½ cups frozen and thawed or fresh pitted sweet cherries

1 teaspoon orange zest

2 tablespoons orange juice

2 tablespoons sliced almonds

1 Preheat oven to 350 degrees F. Place butter in a 9-inch deep-dish pie plate or a 1-½ quart baking dish and put in oven to melt.

2 Meanwhile, in a large bowl, stir together flour, baking powder, and salt. Stir in milk, sugar, and vanilla. In another bowl, mix together cherries, orange zest, and orange juice.

3 Carefully remove pie plate from oven, pour in batter and top with cherry mixture. Sprinkle almonds over top and bake 30 minutes or until fruit is bubbly and edges are golden brown.

Tina's Tip: *To make this even more decadent, top each portion with a nice scoop of vanilla ice cream.*

This delicious cobbler is made with one of my dad's favorite dessert combinations: cherries and nuts. Whenever I make it, I think of him. It's a quick and easy dessert that is great for cozy nights in. Sometimes, I even catch myself staring into the oven as it bakes—it's pretty neat to see the batter rise up around the fruit. Hey, I said "sometimes"!

Shortbread Cookie Banana Pudding

Serves 12 to 15

1 (10-ounce) package shortbread cookies

1 tablespoon lemon juice

1 cup water

5 bananas, cut into ¼-inch-thick slices

1-½ cups milk

1 (4-serving-size) package instant French vanilla pudding mix

1 (8-ounce) package cream cheese, softened

1 (14-ounce) can sweetened condensed milk

1 (8-ounce) container frozen whipped topping, thawed (see Tip)

1 Line the bottom of a 9- x 13-inch baking dish with a single layer of cookies. (There will be extra for garnish.)

2 In a medium bowl, mix lemon juice and water. Add bananas and toss well. Remove bananas from bowl and place on paper towels; pat dry. Layer bananas on top of cookies, overlapping; set aside.

3 In a medium bowl with an electric mixer, beat milk and pudding mix until smooth; refrigerate 5 minutes.

4 In another bowl beat cream cheese and condensed milk until smooth. Fold whipped topping into cream cheese mixture. Add cream cheese mixture to pudding mixture and stir until well combined.

5 Pour pudding mixture over cookies and bananas. Crumble remaining cookies and sprinkle over top. Refrigerate at least 3 hours or until ready to serve.

Tina's Tip: *If you want to create a really impressive presentation, you can layer this in a trifle dish or make individual ones in mason jars.*

My family loves going to BBQ restaurants. And you can bet that if there is banana pudding on the menu, my girls always order it. But we don't always wait to go to a restaurant to enjoy it. I'll make it at home from time to time. It's fun to recreate our favorites, and when I do, I give it my own special twist.

From-Scratch Sweet Dough

Makes 1 batch

1 stick butter

½ cup milk

½ cup warm water
(about 105 degrees F)

1 (.25-ounce) packet instant/
rapid rise yeast (2-¼ teaspoons)

⅓ cup sugar

1 large egg

3 large egg yolks

1 teaspoon vanilla

5 cups all-purpose flour, divided

1-¼ teaspoons salt

Oil for greasing bowl

Tina's Tip: *If you don't have a great warm place for your dough to rise, create one by heating up some water and placing the dough in the oven (turned off) on an upper rack. Place an empty, heat-safe dish on a lower oven rack. Pour a few cups of hot water into the empty dish and close the oven door. This creates a warm, steamy environment for the dough to rise.*

1 In a saucepan over low heat, heat butter and milk until butter is melted; allow to cool slightly. In a stand mixer bowl with a flat beater attached, add warm water, yeast, sugar, egg, yolks, and vanilla; mix on low until combined.

2 Slowly add 4 cups flour and salt; mix on low until flour is combined, then increase speed to 2-3 and drizzle in milk mixture. Mix until dough starts to pull together. (Dough will still be quite wet.)

3 Switch from flat beater to dough hook and knead on speed 2, adding ½ cup of flour, 1 tablespoon at a time, until dough is smooth and pulls away from bowl. (I use about ¾ of remaining flour.) Knead about 5 more minutes. (The dough should be soft and will cling to/ride up the dough hook.) Stop and scrape the dough off the dough hook a few times during the kneading process.

4 Lightly oil a large bowl. Place dough in bowl, turning dough over so oiled side of dough is facing up. Cover bowl with plastic wrap and place in a warm place (see Tip) until dough has doubled in size, about 2 hours.

Wondering what to make with this dough? You can use it to make my Fluffy Overnight Cinnamon Rolls (page 11) or Party Time Beignets (page 221).

Party Time Beignets

Makes about 5 dozen

1 batch From-Scratch
Sweet Dough (see page 220)

2 cups vegetable shortening
or oil

Powdered sugar for sprinkling

Tina's Tip: *These are great on their own, but they're even more amazing when you serve them with coffee, hot chocolate, or a warmed dipping sauce (like caramel or chocolate sauce).*

1 Lightly flour a cutting board and with a floured rolling pin, roll out dough to an 8- x 16-inch rectangle. Cut into 2-inch squares.

2 In a large, deep skillet over medium heat, heat shortening or oil until hot, but not smoking. Add dough squares, a few at a time, and cook in batches, about 30 seconds per side or until golden. Remove with a slotted spoon and drain on a paper towel-lined baking sheet.

3 While warm, sprinkle beignets generously with powdered sugar. Serve warm.

There's a local restaurant that my family and I like to go to that sells mini doughnuts coated in cinnamon sugar, and they serve them with caramel sauce. They're simply amazing and were the inspiration for these beignets. Coincidentally, this restaurant was also where I got the idea to add a caramel dipping sauce to my winning recipe in the Pillsbury Bake-Off® Contest.

No-Churn Cookies & Cream Ice Cream

Serves 6 to 8

2 cups heavy cream

1 teaspoon vanilla

1 (14-ounce) can sweetened condensed milk

15 chocolate crème-filled sandwich cookies, coarsely chopped

1 In a large bowl with an electric mixer, beat heavy cream until it just starts to thicken. Add vanilla and slowly add ¼ of the can of sweetened condensed milk. Continue to whip until well incorporated. Repeat adding another ¼ of the sweetened condensed milk and whipping it until it has all been added. Continue whipping until mixture has thickened, increased in volume, and formed soft peaks.

2 With a rubber spatula, gently stir in cookies.

3 Spoon mixture into a 9- x 5-inch loaf pan. Cover with plastic wrap and freeze 6 to 8 hours or until firm. Then grab an ice cream scoop and dig in.

Tina's Tip: *You can get as creative as you like! Adjust the flavorings or add in your favorite mix-ins—anything from chopped nuts to mini chocolate chips. It's your ice cream, so there are no rules.*

We're all big fans of homemade ice cream at our house. With this recipe you don't even need an ice cream maker to enjoy creamy and rich ice cream. This ice cream is perfect for eating out of a bowl on its own, or for serving with all of your pies, crumbles, crisps, and cobblers (a la mode-style!).

Homemade Buttercream Frosting

Makes about 3-1/2 cups, enough for 24 cupcakes or 1 (8- to 9-inch) 2-layer cake

1-½ sticks butter, softened

1 pinch salt

½ teaspoon vanilla

6 cups powdered sugar

¼ cup milk

1 In a large bowl with an electric mixer on medium speed, beat butter until smooth and fluffy. Add salt and vanilla, and gradually mix in 2 cups of sugar. Add 1 tablespoon milk, then continue adding sugar and milk 1 tablespoon at a time to reach desired consistency. Mix until smooth and creamy.

I have been making this style of frosting for as long as I can remember. It's the type my Mom always made, but she used less butter and always called it "icing." On occasion, I'll make the fancier Italian buttercream that my niece, Valerie, (who is a pastry chef) taught me. But this American-style buttercream is what I grew up with and the frosting my family loves.

Cream Cheese Frosting

Makes about 3-1/2 cups, enough for 24 cupcakes or 1 (8- to 9-inch) 2-layer cake

1 (8-ounce) package cream cheese, softened

½ stick butter, softened

½ teaspoon vanilla

1 teaspoon milk, plus more if needed

6 cups powdered sugar

1 In a large bowl with an electric mixer on medium speed, beat cream cheese and butter until smooth and fluffy. Add vanilla and 1 teaspoon milk, and gradually add sugar. If the frosting seems too thick, add a little more milk. Mix until smooth and creamy.

Tina's Tip: *This frosting can be refrigerated or frozen until you're ready to use it. Right before using, thaw (if frozen) and use a mixer to beat until it's fluffy.*

This is one of my favorite frostings. It's easy to whip together and delicious on cinnamon rolls and almost any cake!

DESSERT

Make-Ahead Whipped Cream

Makes 3-1/2 to 4 cups

2 cups very cold heavy whipping cream

2 tablespoons instant vanilla pudding mix

½ teaspoon vanilla

⅓ cup powdered sugar

1 Using an electric mixer with a whisk accessory or by hand, start whipping the cold cream and pudding mix on low speed. When mixture starts to thicken, add remaining ingredients, slowly increasing speed and keep whipping till you reach the desired consistency. (I suggest until stiff peaks form.)

Chocolate Version: *Omit the powdered sugar and add ⅓ cup chocolate syrup.*

Strawberry Version: *Omit the powdered sugar and add ½ cup strawberry jelly or jam, and a drop of red food coloring, if desired.*

Candy Cane Version: *Omit the vanilla and add 1-¼ teaspoons peppermint extract and a drop of red food coloring. After whipping, sprinkle with 2 tablespoons of crushed peppermint candy.*

Tina's Tip: *You can chill the beaters and bowl in your refrigerator for faster whipping. This can be made a day in advance and stored in the refrigerator in an airtight container.*

Adding a little instant pudding mix to your whipped cream helps keep it from weeping, so you can make it ahead of time. This whipped cream also makes for a yummy light and not-too-sweet frosting! I use this in a lot of recipes that call for frozen whipped topping.

Sweet & Salty Snack Mix

Serves 6 to 8

8 cups popped popcorn

2 cups mini pretzels

1 cup candy-coated chocolate pieces

¼ cup sprinkles

¾ cup dried cranberries

8 ounces white chocolate melting wafers, chips, or squares

1 In a large bowl, combine popcorn, pretzels, candy-coated chocolates, sprinkles, and dried cranberries; mix well.

2 In a medium, microwave-safe bowl, melt white chocolate 30 seconds. Stir and repeat until chocolate is melted and smooth. (Do not overheat.) Pour chocolate over popcorn mixture and toss until evenly coated.

3 Spread onto a large, rimmed baking sheet. Let cool completely, then break up into chunks. Store in an airtight container.

The first time I had a snack mix like this was at a friend's wedding. The bridesmaids and I were munching while we helped get the bride ready. It was so good, we couldn't stop! Now I make this at home and keep some stored away. That way, I can reach for it whenever I get a craving for a sweet and salty snack.

Notes

Notes

Notes

Recipes in Alphabetical Order

All-American Mac & Cheese 144

Asparagus & Bacon Cheesy Quiche............. 10

Avocado Toast Eggs Benedict 8

Bacon-Wrapped Barbecue Shrimp 40

Bacon-Wrapped Green Bean Bundles 164

Balsamic Veggie Stacks 158

Barbecue Chicken Waffle Sliders 26

Barbecued Baby Back Ribs 129

Bee's Knees Blue Cheese Spread 50

Best-of-Both-Worlds Potato Salad 179

Bite-Sized Shrimp Egg Rolls 30

Black Forest Dump Cake...........................202

Brown Sugar Glazed Salmon 136

Brown Sugar Grilled Pineapple.................. 172

Bundt Pan Roasted Chicken 91

Busy Weeknight Tortilla Soup 64

Caprese Orzo Salad................................. 176

Cheddar-Bacon Deviled Eggs....................... 42

Cheddar-Crusted Cottage Pie.................... 114

Cheddar-Stuffed Yeast Rolls..................... 188

Cheesy Broccoli "Tots".............................. 35

Cheesy Cauliflower and Potato Mash 174

Cheesy Chicken & Pimiento Melts 74

Cheesy Sausage Stuffed Shells.................. 148

Cherry Cobbler with Orange & Almonds 217

Chianti & Rosemary Beef Stew 111

Chicken Enchilada Dip 52

Chicken Rigatoni with Creamy Marinara 146

Chicken Salad Lettuce Wraps...................... 66

Chili Butter Corn on the Cob 168

Chocolate Chip & Raspberry Brownies........206

Chocolate Layer Birthday Cake 196

Chocolate-Almond Crescent Rollups.............19

Chocolate-Covered Cookie Butter Balls..... 210

Chunky Chicken Noodle Soup 60

Cinnamon Crumble Apple Pie.................... 214

Coconut Curry Chicken Skewers.................. 94

Cornbread Taco Casserole........................... 92

Crab Cake Pepper Poppers........................... 34

Cranberry Brie Pull-Apart Bread 46

Cream Cheese Frosting................................224

Cream Cheese Pound Cake 195

Creamy Broccoli & Cheddar Soup 58

Creamy Lemon Shrimp 140

Creamy Risotto Carbonara 186

Crispy Crunchy Croutons............................. 72

Crispy-Coated Crab Cakes........................ 134

Dill-icious Oven-Fried Chicken 88

Easy Buttermilk Ranch Dressing 72

Easy Classic Pizza Dough.......................... 153

Easy Egg Roll in a Bowl 128

Egg Salad BLT Sandwiches 76

Farmer's Market Spinach Salad.................... 69

Fig, Prosciutto, and Arugula Flatbread 156

Flavorful Turkey Brine 103

Fluffy & Creamy No-Bake Cheesecake 194

Fluffy Overnight Cinnamon Rolls 11

Foil Packet Pierogi Dinner 125

Fri-Yay Fish Tacos 139

From-Scratch Sweet Dough 220

Fudge-Filled Ice Cream Cupcakes 200

Garlic-Parmesan Brussels Sprouts 166

Greek Isles Breakfast Wraps.........................6

Greek-Style Grouper 138

Grilled Steak Mediterranean Salad 65

Hearty Ham & Potato Hash 7

Herb-Brined Roasted Turkey...................... 102

Homemade Buttercream Frosting 224

Homemade Spaetzle................................. 178

Honey-Garlic Pork Tenderloin 123

Horseradish-Kissed Pot Roast 112

Italian-Stuffed Chicken Cutlets 99

Italian-Style Quinoa Bowls 70

Just Peachy Bourbon Spread........................ 15

Recipes in Alphabetical Order

Lemon-Kissed Raspberry Muffins 20

Loaded Buffalo Chicken Meatballs 32

Lou's Favorite Thai Chili Wings 28

Make-Ahead Whipped Cream 225

Mama Mia's Meatball Pizza 154

Marinated Cucumber Salad 169

Mattison Avenue Toffee Cheesecake.......... 192

Maui BBQ Chicken 96

Meatball & Ricotta Hoagies 116

My Go-To Meatloaf 108

My Mom's Super Sandwiches 78

My Mom's Homemade Brownies 205

My Perfect Pie Crust Dough......................... 215

No-Churn Cookies & Cream Ice Cream....... 222

Not-Your-Everyday Cornbread Stuffing...... 182

One-Pan Parmesan Chicken 82

Open-Faced Portobello

   "Steak" Sandwiches 77

Open-Faced Steakhouse Special 118

Our Favorite Pancakes 12

Parmesan Turkey Patties 100

Party-Time Beignets...................................... 221

PB & B Overnight Oats 18

Peachy Blueberry Crisp 216

Peanut Butter S'mores Cookie Bars............ 208

Pecan Streusel French Toast Cups 2

Pennsylvania Dutch Chicken & Dumplings ... 90

Pesto & Peppers Cheese Tortellini 150

Poached Shrimp with Tropical Fruit Salsa .. 132

Potato-Crusted Pork Chops 126

Quick Pickled Red Onions............................. 44

Ramen Noodle Steak Bowl 106

Roasted Country Vegetables....................... 162

Roasted Pork with

   Pineapple-Pepper Jelly............................. 122

Rosemary Lemon Smashed Potatoes 184

Salami & Fontina Hamburgers 120

Salmon Caesar Salad 68

Salted Pecan Pie Bars 204

Sheet Pan Chicken Supper 86

Shortbread Cookie Banana Pudding.......... 218

Simmering Greek Chicken 98

Simple Lentil Soup 61

Skillet Chicken & White Wine Mushrooms 95

Slow Cooker Balsamic Chicken 84

Slow Cooker Chili Soup 56

Slow Cooker Sausage & Bean One-Pot 124

Smoky & Sweet Baked Beans 170

Southern "Fried" Pickles 36

Spinach-Artichoke Mini Potato Skins........... 38

Spiralized Sweet Potato Bake.........................4

Strawberry Shortcake Waffles 16

Strawberry Sunrise Smoothie....................... 22

Strawberry-Lemon Poke Cake 198

Street Corn Layer Dip................................... 48

"Stuffed Mushroom" Florentine Soup 62

Supreme Stuffed Portobello Mushrooms ... 152

Sweet & Salty Snack Mix 226

Sweet & Sour Short Ribs with Cabbage 117

Sweet & Spicy Candied Bacon 14

Taste of Tuscany Grilled Cheese................... 73

Three-in-One Homemade Pasta 142

Touch-of-Honey Sweet Potato Mash.......... 180

Triple Chocolate Biscotti.............................. 211

Tropical Summer Smoothie 22

Unstuffed Stuffed Pepper Casserole.......... 110

Veggie Lover's Lasagna 147

Weeknight-Friendly Chicken Cacciatore....... 87

White Bean Hummus Crostini 43

White Chocolate Chip

   Peanut Butter Cookies 212

Recipes by Category

Appetizers

See Chapter Table of Contents 25

Bacon

Asparagus & Bacon Cheesy Quiche........... 10
Bacon-Wrapped Barbecue Shrimp 40
Bacon-Wrapped Green Bean Bundles 164
Bee's Knees Blue Cheese Spread 50
Cheddar-Bacon Deviled Eggs.................... 42
Creamy Risotto Carbonara 186
Egg Salad BLT Sandwiches........................ 76
Not-Your-Everyday Cornbread Stuffing 182
Potato-Crusted Pork Chops 126
Sweet & Spicy Candied Bacon 14

Beans

Cornbread Taco Casserole........................ 92
Slow Cooker Chili Soup............................ 56
Slow Cooker Sausage & Bean One-Pot..... 124
Smoky & Sweet Baked Beans 170
Street Corn Layer Dip 48
White Bean Hummus Crostini 43

Beef

Cheddar-Crusted Cottage Pie.................. 114
Chianti & Rosemary Beef Stew 111
Grilled Steak Mediterranean Salad 65
Horseradish-Kissed Pot Roast 112
Mama Mia's Meatball Pizza 154
Meatball & Ricotta Hoagies 116
My Go-To Meatloaf 108
Open-Faced Steakhouse Special 118
Ramen Noodle Steak Bowl 106
Salami & Fontina Hamburgers 120
Simple Lentil Soup................................... 61
Slow Cooker Chili Soup............................ 56
Sweet & Sour Short Ribs with Cabbage 117
Unstuffed Stuffed Pepper Casserole........ 110

Bread

All-American Mac & Cheese 144
Avocado Toast Eggs Benedict 8
Busy Weeknight Tortilla Soup 64

Cheddar-Stuffed Yeast Rolls..................... 188
Cheesy Chicken & Pimiento Melts 74
Cornbread Taco Casserole.......................... 92
Cranberry Brie Pull-Apart Bread 46
Crispy Crunchy Croutons 72
Crispy-Coated Crab Cakes 134
Easy Classic Pizza Dough 153
Egg Salad BLT Sandwiches........................ 76
Fig, Prosciutto, and Arugula Flatbread 156
Fluffy Overnight Cinnamon Rolls 11
Fri-Yay Fish Tacos 139
From-Scratch Sweet Dough 220
Garlic-Parmesan Brussels Sprouts 166
Italian-Stuffed Chicken Cutlets 99
Lemon-Kissed Raspberry Muffins.............. 20
Mama Mia's Meatball Pizza 154
Meatball & Ricotta Hoagies...................... 116
My Go-To Meatloaf 108
My Mom's Super Sandwiches 78
Not-Your-Everyday Cornbread Stuffing.... 182
Open-Faced Portobello
  "Steak" Sandwiches............................... 77
Open-Faced Steakhouse Special 118
Parmesan Turkey Patties.......................... 100
Party-Time Beignets.............................. 221
Pecan Streusel French Toast Cups 2
Pennsylvania Dutch
  Chicken & Dumplings 90
Salami & Fontina Hamburgers 120
Salmon Caesar Salad 68
"Stuffed Mushroom" Florentine Soup 62
Supreme Stuffed
  Portobello Mushrooms........................... 152
Taste of Tuscany Grilled Cheese 73
White Bean Hummus Crostini 43

Breakfast

See Chapter Table of Contents 1

Brownies/Bars

Chocolate Chip & Raspberry Brownies......206
My Mom's Homemade Brownies.............205

Recipes by Category

Peanut Butter S'mores Cookie Bars 208
Salted Pecan Pie Bars 204

Cakes/Cupcakes/Cheesecakes

Black Forest Dump Cake 202
Chocolate Layer Birthday Cake 196
Cream Cheese Pound Cake 195
Fluffy & Creamy No-Bake Cheesecake 194
Fudge-Filled Ice Cream Cupcakes 200
Mattison Avenue Toffee Cheesecake 192
Strawberry-Lemon Poke Cake 198

Casseroles

All-American Mac & Cheese 144
Cheddar-Crusted Cottage Pie 114
Cheesy Sausage Stuffed Shells 148
Cornbread Taco Casserole 92
Not-Your-Everyday Cornbread Stuffing 182
Smoky & Sweet Baked Beans 170
Spiralized Sweet Potato Bake 4
Unstuffed Stuffed Pepper Casserole 110
Veggie Lover's Lasagna 147

Cheese

All-American Mac & Cheese 144
Asparagus & Bacon Cheesy Quiche 10
Balsamic Veggie Stacks 158
Barbecue Chicken Waffle Sliders 26
Bee's Knees Blue Cheese Spread 50
Black Forest Dump Cake 202
Busy Weeknight Tortilla Soup 64
Caprese Orzo Salad 176
Cheddar-Bacon Deviled Eggs 42
Cheddar-Crusted Cottage Pie 114
Cheddar-Stuffed Yeast Rolls 188
Cheesy Broccoli "Tots" 35
Cheesy Cauliflower and Potato Mash 174
Cheesy Chicken & Pimiento Melts 74
Cheesy Sausage Stuffed Shells 148
Chicken Enchilada Dip 52
Chicken Rigatoni with Creamy Marinara ... 146
Cranberry Brie Pull-Apart Bread 46
Cream Cheese Frosting 224

Cream Cheese Pound Cake 195
Creamy Broccoli & Cheddar Soup 58
Creamy Risotto Carbonara 186
Dill-icious Oven-Fried Chicken 88
Farmer's Market Spinach Salad 69
Fig, Prosciutto, and Arugula Flatbread 156
Fluffy & Creamy No-Bake Cheesecake 194
Garlic-Parmesan Brussels Sprouts 166
Greek Isles Breakfast Wraps 6
Greek-Style Grouper 138
Grilled Steak Mediterranean Salad 65
Italian-Stuffed Chicken Cutlets 99
Italian-Style Quinoa Bowls 70
Loaded Buffalo Chicken Meatballs 32
Mama Mia's Meatball Pizza 154
Mattison Avenue Toffee Cheesecake 192
Maui BBQ Chicken 96
Meatball & Ricotta Hoagies 116
My Mom's Super Sandwiches 78
One-Pan Parmesan Chicken 82
Open-Faced Portobello
  "Steak" Sandwiches 77
Parmesan Turkey Patties 100
Pesto & Peppers Cheese Tortellini 150
Potato-Crusted Pork Chops 126
Salami & Fontina Hamburgers 120
Salmon Caesar Salad 68
Simmering Greek Chicken 98
Slow Cooker Sausage & Bean One-Pot 124
Spinach-Artichoke Mini Potato Skins 38
Spiralized Sweet Potato Bake 4
Street Corn Layer Dip 48
"Stuffed Mushroom" Florentine Soup 62
Supreme Stuffed
  Portobello Mushrooms 152
Taste of Tuscany Grilled Cheese 73
Unstuffed Stuffed Pepper Casserole 110
Veggie Lover's Lasagna 147

Recipes
by Category

Chocolate

Black Forest Dump Cake 202
Chocolate Chip & Raspberry Brownies......206
Chocolate Layer Birthday Cake 196
Chocolate-Covered Cookie Butter Balls ...210
Fudge-Filled Ice Cream Cupcakes 200
Mattison Avenue Toffee Cheesecake........192
My Mom's Homemade Brownies.................205
No-Churn Cookies & Cream Ice Cream.....222
Peanut Butter S'mores Cookie Bars 208
Sweet & Salty Snack Mix..........................226
Triple Chocolate Biscotti 211
White Chocolate Chip
    Peanut Butter Cookies 212

Cookies

Chocolate-Covered Cookie Butter Balls ...210
Triple Chocolate Biscotti 211
White Chocolate Chip
    Peanut Butter Cookies 212

Desserts

See Chapter Table of Contents 191

Eggs

Asparagus & Bacon Cheesy Quiche........... 10
Avocado Toast Eggs Benedict 8
Cheddar-Bacon Deviled Eggs..................... 42
Egg Salad BLT Sandwiches......................... 76
Greek Isles Breakfast Wraps 6
Best-of-Both-Worlds Potato Salad 179
Ramen Noodle Steak Bowl 106
Spiralized Sweet Potato Bake........................4

Fish

Brown Sugar Glazed Salmon..................... 136
Fri-Yay Fish Tacos 139
Greek-Style Grouper 138
Salmon Caesar Salad 68

Fruit

Avocado Toast Eggs Benedict 8
Black Forest Dump Cake 202
Brown Sugar Grilled Pineapple................. 172

Cherry Cobbler with Orange & Almonds ... 217
Chicken Salad Lettuce Wraps 66
Chili Butter Corn on the Cob 168
Chocolate Chip & Raspberry Brownies......206
Cinnamon Crumble Apple Pie................... 214
Cranberry Brie Pull-Apart Bread 46
Creamy Lemon Shrimp 140
Farmer's Market Spinach Salad.................. 69
Fig, Prosciutto, and Arugula Flatbread 156
Flavorful Turkey Brine............................... 103
Herb-Brined Roasted Turkey 102
Honey-Garlic Pork Tenderloin 123
Just Peachy Bourbon Spread 15
Maui BBQ Chicken 96
Peachy Blueberry Crisp.............................. 216
Poached Shrimp with Tropical
    Fruit Salsa 132
Roasted Pork with
    Pineapple-Pepper Jelly.......................... 122
Rosemary Lemon Smashed Potatoes 184
Shortbread Cookie Banana Pudding......... 218
Strawberry-Lemon Poke Cake 198
Sweet & Salty Snack Mix.......................... 226
Unstuffed Stuffed Pepper Casserole........ 110

Grains

Creamy Risotto Carbonara 186
Italian-Style Quinoa Bowls.......................... 70
Peachy Blueberry Crisp.............................. 216
Simple Lentil Soup 61
Unstuffed Stuffed Pepper Casserole........ 110

Nuts

Bee's Knees Blue Cheese Spread 50
Cherry Cobbler with Orange & Almonds ... 217
Chicken Salad Lettuce Wraps 66
Chocolate-Almond Crescent Rollups...........19
Pecan Streusel French Toast Cups 2
Pesto & Peppers Cheese Tortellini 150
Salted Pecan Pie Bars............................... 204

Recipes by Category

Pasta

All-American Mac & Cheese 144
Caprese Orzo Salad 176
Cheesy Sausage Stuffed Shells............. 148
Chicken Rigatoni with Creamy Marinara ... 146
Chunky Chicken Noodle Soup 60
Creamy Lemon Shrimp 140
Homemade Spaetzle 178
Pesto & Peppers Cheese Tortellini 150
Ramen Noodle Steak Bowl 106
Slow Cooker Sausage & Bean One-Pot..... 124
Three-in-One Homemade Pasta 142
Veggie Lover's Lasagna 147

Peanut Butter

Coconut Curry Chicken Skewers 94
PB & B Overnight Oats......................... 18
Peanut Butter S'mores Cookie Bars..........208
White Chocolate Chip
   Peanut Butter Cookies............................ 212

Pies

Cinnamon Crumble Apple Pie..................... 214
Fluffy & Creamy No-Bake Cheesecake..... 194
My Perfect Pie Crust Dough 215

Pizza

Easy Classic Pizza Dough 153
Fig, Prosciutto, and Arugula Flatbread 156
Mama Mia's Meatball Pizza 154

Pork

Asparagus & Bacon Cheesy Quiche............ 10
Bacon-Wrapped Barbecue Shrimp 40
Bacon-Wrapped Green Bean Bundles 164
Bee's Knees Blue Cheese Spread 50
Cheddar-Bacon Deviled Eggs..................... 42
Creamy Risotto Carbonara 186
Easy Egg Roll in a Bowl 128
Egg Salad BLT Sandwiches......................... 76
Fig, Prosciutto, and Arugula Flatbread..... 156
Foil Packet Pierogi Dinner......................... 125
Hearty Ham & Potato Hash 7

Honey-Garlic Pork Tenderloin 123
My Mom's Super Sandwiches 78
Not-Your-Everyday Cornbread Stuffing.... 182
Potato-Crusted Pork Chops 126
Roasted Pork with
   Pineapple-Pepper Jelly......................... 122
Salami & Fontina Hamburgers 120
Slow Cooker Sausage & Bean One-Pot..... 124
"Stuffed Mushroom" Florentine Soup 62
Supreme Stuffed
   Portobello Mushrooms..................... 152
Sweet & Spicy Candied Bacon 14

Potatoes

Cheddar-Crusted Cottage Pie................... 114
Cheesy Cauliflower and Potato Mash 174
Hearty Ham & Potato Hash 7
Potato-Crusted Pork Chops 126
Best-of-Both-Worlds Potato Salad 179
Rosemary Lemon Smashed Potatoes 184
Sheet Pan Chicken Supper 86
Spinach-Artichoke Mini Potato Skins.......... 38
Spiralized Sweet Potato Bake.........................4
Touch-of-Honey Sweet Potato Mash........ 180

Poultry

Barbecue Chicken Waffle Sliders................. 26
Bundt Pan Roasted Chicken 91
Busy Weeknight Tortilla Soup 64
Cheesy Chicken & Pimiento Melts 74
Cheesy Sausage Stuffed Shells................. 148
Chicken Enchilada Dip 52
Chicken Rigatoni with Creamy Marinara ... 146
Chicken Salad Lettuce Wraps 66
Chunky Chicken Noodle Soup 60
Coconut Curry Chicken Skewers 94
Cornbread Taco Casserole......................... 92
Creamy Broccoli & Cheddar Soup 58
Creamy Risotto Carbonara 186
Dill-icious Oven-Fried Chicken................... 88
Flavorful Turkey Brine............................. 103
Herb-Brined Roasted Turkey................... 102

Recipes
by Category

Italian-Stuffed Chicken Cutlets 99
Loaded Buffalo Chicken Meatballs 32
Lou's Favorite Thai Chili Wings................... 28
Maui BBQ Chicken 96
Not-Your-Everyday Cornbread Stuffing.... 182
One-Pan Parmesan Chicken 82
Parmesan Turkey Patties........................ 100
Pennsylvania Dutch
  Chicken & Dumplings 90
Sheet Pan Chicken Supper 86
Simmering Greek Chicken 98
Skillet Chicken & White Wine Mushrooms .. 95
Slow Cooker Balsamic Chicken 84
Slow Cooker Sausage & Bean One-Pot..... 124
Spiralized Sweet Potato Bake.........................4
"Stuffed Mushroom" Florentine Soup 62
Weeknight-Friendly Chicken Cacciatore..... 87

Rice
Creamy Risotto Carbonara 186
Unstuffed Stuffed Pepper Casserole........ 110

Salads
Caprese Orzo Salad 176
Chicken Salad Lettuce Wraps 66
Farmer's Market Spinach Salad.................. 69
Grilled Steak Mediterranean Salad 65
Italian-Style Quinoa Bowls 70
Best-of-Both-Worlds Potato Salad 179
Salmon Caesar Salad 68

Sandwiches
Cheesy Chicken & Pimiento Melts 74
Egg Salad BLT Sandwiches........................ 76
Meatball & Ricotta Hoagies...................... 116
My Mom's Super Sandwiches 78
Open-Faced Portobello
  "Steak" Sandwiches................................ 77
Open-Faced Steakhouse Special 118
Salami & Fontina Hamburgers 120
Taste of Tuscany Grilled Cheese 73

Shellfish
Bite-Sized Shrimp Egg Rolls 30
Bacon-Wrapped Barbecue Shrimp 40
Crab Cake Pepper Poppers....................... 34
Creamy Lemon Shrimp 140
Crispy-Coated Crab Cakes 134
Poached Shrimp with
  Tropical Fruit Salsa............................... 132

Side Dishes
See Chapter Table of Contents 161

Slow Cooker
Slow Cooker Balsamic Chicken 84
Slow Cooker Chili Soup.............................. 56
Slow Cooker Sausage & Bean One-Pot..... 124

Soups
Busy Weeknight Tortilla Soup 64
Chianti & Rosemary Beef Stew.................. 111
Chunky Chicken Noodle Soup 60
Creamy Broccoli & Cheddar Soup 58
Simple Lentil Soup.................................... 61
Slow Cooker Chili Soup.............................. 56
Slow Cooker Sausage & Bean One-Pot..... 124
"Stuffed Mushroom" Florentine Soup 62

Spirits / Liquours / Beers
Bundt Pan Roasted Chicken 91
Chianti & Rosemary Beef Stew.................. 111
Chicken Rigatoni with Creamy Marinara ... 146
Creamy Lemon Shrimp 140
Just Peachy Bourbon Spread 15
"Stuffed Mushroom" Florentine Soup 62
Skillet Chicken & White Wine Mushrooms .. 95
Weeknight-Friendly Chicken Cacciatore..... 87

Vegetables
Asparagus & Bacon Cheesy Quiche........... 10
Bacon-Wrapped Green Bean Bundles 164
Balsamic Veggie Stacks........................... 158
Barbecue Chicken Waffle Sliders 26
Bee's Knees Blue Cheese Spread 50
Bite-Sized Shrimp Egg Rolls 30

Recipes
by Category

Bundt Pan Roasted Chicken 91

Busy Weeknight Tortilla Soup 64

Caprese Orzo Salad 176

Cheddar-Bacon Deviled Eggs.................... 42

Cheddar-Crusted Cottage Pie.................... 114

Cheesy Broccoli "Tots" 35

Cheesy Cauliflower and Potato Mash 174

Cheesy Chicken & Pimiento Melts 74

Cheesy Sausage Stuffed Shells................. 148

Chianti & Rosemary Beef Stew 111

Chicken Enchilada Dip 52

Chicken Salad Lettuce Wraps 66

Chili Butter Corn on the Cob 168

Chunky Chicken Noodle Soup 60

Cornbread Taco Casserole........................ 92

Crab Cake Pepper Poppers........................ 34

Creamy Broccoli & Cheddar Soup 58

Creamy Lemon Shrimp 140

Creamy Risotto Carbonara 186

Crispy-Coated Crab Cakes 134

Easy Egg Roll in a Bowl 128

Egg Salad BLT Sandwiches........................ 76

Farmer's Market Spinach Salad.................. 69

Fig, Prosciutto, and Arugula Flatbread 156

Foil Packet Pierogi Dinner........................ 125

Fri-Yay Fish Tacos 139

Garlic-Parmesan Brussels Sprouts 166

Greek Isles Breakfast Wraps 6

Greek-Style Grouper 138

Grilled Steak Mediterranean Salad 65

Hearty Ham & Potato Hash 7

Herb-Brined Roasted Turkey.................... 102

Horseradish-Kissed Pot Roast 112

Italian-Stuffed Chicken Cutlets 99

Italian-Style Quinoa Bowls........................ 70

Loaded Buffalo Chicken Meatballs 32

Marinated Cucumber Salad....................... 169

Maui BBQ Chicken 96

My Go-To Meatloaf 108

Not-Your-Everyday Cornbread Stuffing.... 182

One-Pan Parmesan Chicken 82

Open-Faced Portobello
   "Steak" Sandwiches................................. 77

Open-Faced Steakhouse Special 118

Parmesan Turkey Patties.......................... 100

Pennsylvania Dutch
   Chicken & Dumplings 90

Pesto & Peppers Cheese Tortellini 150

Poached Shrimp with
   Tropical Fruit Salsa................................. 132

Best-of-Both-Worlds Potato Salad 179

Quick Pickled Red Onions......................... 44

Ramen Noodle Steak Bowl 106

Roasted Country Vegetables.................... 162

Rosemary Lemon Smashed Potatoes 184

Salami & Fontina Hamburgers 120

Salmon Caesar Salad 68

Sheet Pan Chicken Supper 86

Simmering Greek Chicken 98

Simple Lentil Soup...................................... 61

Skillet Chicken & White Wine
   Mushrooms... 95

Slow Cooker Balsamic Chicken 84

Slow Cooker Chili Soup 56

Slow Cooker Sausage & Bean One-Pot..... 124

Smoky & Sweet Baked Beans 170

Southern "Fried" Pickles 36

Spinach-Artichoke Mini Potato Skins.......... 38

Spiralized Sweet Potato Bake.......................4

Street Corn Layer Dip 48

"Stuffed Mushroom" Florentine Soup 62

Supreme Stuffed
   Portobello Mushrooms............................. 152

Sweet & Sour Short Ribs with Cabbage 117

Taste of Tuscany Grilled Cheese 73

Touch-of-Honey Sweet Potato Mash........ 180

Unstuffed Stuffed Pepper Casserole........ 110

Veggie Lover's Lasagna 147

Weeknight-Friendly Chicken Cacciatore..... 87

White Bean Hummus Crostini 43